UNLOCK

Second Edition

1

Listening, Speaking & Critical Thinking

STUDENT'S BOOK

N.M. White, Susan Peterson and Nancy Jordan
with Chris Sowton, Jessica Williams,
Christina Cavage and Kimberly Russell

CAMBRIDGE
UNIVERSITY PRESS

CAMBRIDGE
UNIVERSITY PRESS

University Printing House, Cambridge CB2 8BS, United Kingdom

One Liberty Plaza, 20th Floor, New York, NY 10006, USA

477 Williamstown Road, Port Melbourne, VIC 3207, Australia

314–321, 3rd Floor, Plot 3, Splendor Forum, Jasola District Centre, New Delhi – 110025, India

79 Anson Road, 06–04/06, Singapore 079906

Cambridge University Press is part of the University of Cambridge.

It furthers the University's mission by disseminating knowledge in the pursuit of education, learning and research at the highest international levels of excellence.

www.cambridge.org
Information on this title: www.cambridge.org/9781108567275

First published 2014
Second Edition 2019

20 19 18 17 16 15 14 13 12 11 10 9 8 7 6 5 4 3

Printed in Italy by Rotolito S.p.A.

A catalogue record for this publication is available from the British Library

ISBN 978-1-108-56727-5 Listening, Speaking and Critical Thinking Student's Book, Mobile App & Online Workbook 1 with Downloadable Audio & Video

CONTENTS

UNIT	VIDEO	LISTENING	VOCABULARY	
1 PEOPLE Listening 1: Introductions (Communications) Listening 2: Presentations about famous people (Anthropology)	A clothes maker and a furniture maker in Johannesburg	**_Key listening skills:_** Understanding key vocabulary **_Additional skills:_** Using your knowledge Listening for main ideas Listening for detail **_Pronunciation for listening:_** Syllable stress	Family Jobs Countries and nationalities	
2 SEASONS Listening 1: A talk about different seasons (Meteorology) Listening 2: Presentations about places (Geography)	How deserts are formed	**_Key listening skills:_** Predicting content using visuals **_Additional skills:_** Understanding key vocabulary Using your knowledge Listening for main ideas Listening for detail Synthesizing **_Pronunciation for listening:_** Sentence stress	Seasons Weather Colours Adjectives	
3 LIFESTYLE Listening 1: Conversations about different lifestyles (Sociology) Listening 2: An interview (Anthropology/Education)	Festival of the winds	**_Key listening skills:_** Listening for main ideas **_Additional skills:_** Using your knowledge Understanding key vocabulary Listening for detail Synthesizing **_Pronunciation for listening:_** Intonation in questions and statements	Verb collocations	
4 PLACES Listening 1: A presentation about a new smartphone app (History/Geography) Listening 2: Following directions (Geography)	Shanghai	**_Key listening skills:_** Listening for detail **_Additional skills:_** Understanding key vocabulary Using your knowledge Listening for main ideas Synthesizing **_Pronunciation for listening:_** Stress in directions	Places	

GRAMMAR	CRITICAL THINKING	SPEAKING
Subject pronouns and possessive adjectives The verb *be*	Choosing information for an ideas map	***Preparation for speaking:*** Introducing and starting a talk ***Pronunciation for speaking:*** Syllable stress ***Speaking task:*** Tell your group about a famous person from your country.
There is / There are	Using visuals in a talk	***Preparation for speaking:*** Giving a talk Describing visuals ***Pronunciation for speaking:*** Sentence stress Pauses ***Speaking task:*** Describe photos of a place you want to visit.
The present simple • Statements • Questions	Understanding surveys	***Preparation for speaking:*** Prepositions of time ***Pronunciation for speaking:*** Present simple –s and –es endings ***Speaking task:*** Interview students for a survey.
Prepositions of place The imperative	Interpreting maps and directions	***Preparation for speaking:*** Giving directions Asking for directions ***Pronunciation for speaking:*** Phrases ***Speaking task:*** Ask for and give directions in a university town.

UNIT	VIDEO	LISTENING	VOCABULARY	
5 JOBS Listening 1: A formal conversation asking for advice (Business/Management) Listening 2: A discussion about job applicants (Career Services)	Burj Khalifa	**_Key listening skills:_** Using your knowledge to predict content Listening for opinions **_Additional skills:_** Understanding key vocabulary Using your knowledge Listening for main ideas Listening for detail Synthesizing **_Pronunciation for listening:_** Weak form _have to_	Vocabulary for jobs and workers (_work, job, fit, kind, earn_, etc.)	
6 HOMES AND BUILDINGS Listening 1: A radio interview about restaurants (Architecture) Listening 2: A discussion about buildings (Architecture)	Monticello and Jefferson	**_Key listening skill:_** Listening for reasons **_Additional skills:_** Using your knowledge Understanding key vocabulary Listening for main ideas Listening for detail Synthesizing **_Pronunciation for listening:_** Linking words	Furniture	
7 FOOD AND CULTURE Listening 1: A classroom discussion about food culture (History/Sociology) Listening 2: A student presentation on food culture and changing habits (History/Sociology)	Luxury fruit	**_Key listening skill:_** Listening for numbers **_Additional skills:_** Using your knowledge Understanding key vocabulary Listening for main ideas Listening for detail Predicting content using visuals Synthesizing **_Pronunciation for listening:_** Numbers with _-teen_ and _-ty_	Food	
8 TRANSPORT Listening 1: A talk about the London Underground (Engineering/Urban planning) Listening 2: Two student presentations about traffic problems (Engineering/Urban planning)	China's modern roadways	**_Key listening skill:_** Listening for definitions Synthesizing information **_Additional skills:_** Understanding key vocabulary Using your knowledge Predicting content using visuals Listening for main ideas Listening for detail Taking notes Synthesizing **_Pronunciation for listening:_** Pronouncing years Consonant clusters	Verbs for transport	

GRAMMAR	CRITICAL THINKING	SPEAKING
Have to / has to *Should* Comparative adjectives	Identifying criteria	***Preparation for speaking:*** Comparing Asking for and giving opinions and reasons ***Pronunciation for speaking:*** Weak sounds in comparatives Pronouncing consonants in *have to, have, has to, has* (e.g. /f/, /v/, /z/, /s/) ***Speaking task:*** Choose a person for a job.
Giving an opinion with *should*	Evaluating ideas	***Preparation for speaking:*** Reasons, opinions and agreement • Giving reasons • Giving an opinion • Asking for an opinion • Agreeing and disagreeing ***Speaking task:*** Discuss ideas for a new café.
The past simple 1 • Statements • *Yes/No* questions and short answers • Irregular verbs	Understanding pie charts	***Preparation for speaking:*** Introducing a report Talking about surveys ***Pronunciation for speaking:*** The letter *u* ***Speaking task:*** Report the results of a survey.
The past simple 2 • More irregular verbs *Because / So*	Synthesizing and organizing information for a talk	***Preparation for speaking:*** Describing a topic Describing a problem Describing a solution Describing results ***Pronunciation for speaking:*** *-d / -ed* in regular past simple verbs ***Speaking task:*** Describe a transport problem, solutions and results.

Unlock your academic potential

Unlock Second Edition is a six-level, academic-light English course created to build the skills and language students need for their studies (CEFR Pre-A1 to C1). It develops students' ability to think critically in an academic context right from the start of their language learning. Every level has 100% new inspiring video on a range of academic topics.

Confidence in teaching.
Joy in learning.

Better Learning WITH UNL⌀CK SECOND EDITION

Better Learning is our simple approach where insights we've gained from research have helped shape content that drives results. We've listened to teachers all around the world and made changes so that *Unlock* Second Edition better supports students along the way to academic success.

CRITICAL THINKING

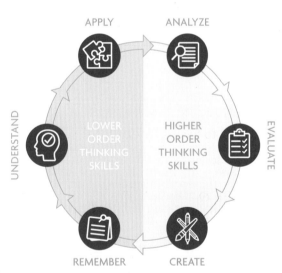

APPLY   ANALYZE

UNDERSTAND

LOWER ORDER THINKING SKILLS   HIGHER ORDER THINKING SKILLS

EVALUATE

REMEMBER   CREATE

Critical thinking in *Unlock* Second Edition ...

- is **informed** by a range of academic research from Bloom in the 1950s, to Krathwohl and Anderson in the 2000s, to more recent considerations relating to 21st Century Skills
- has a **refined** syllabus with a better mix of higher- and lower-order critical thinking skills
- is **measurable**, with objectives and self-evaluation so students can track their critical thinking progress
- is **transparent** so teachers and students know when and why they're developing critical thinking skills
- is **supported** with professional development material for teachers so teachers can teach with confidence

... so that students have the best possible chance of academic success.

INSIGHT

Most classroom time is currently spent on developing lower-order critical thinking skills. Students need to be able to use higher-order critical thinking skills too.

CONTENT

Unlock Second Edition includes the right mix of lower- and higher-order thinking skills development in every unit, with clear learning objectives.

RESULTS

Students are better prepared for their academic studies and have the confidence to apply the critical thinking skills they have developed.

CLASSROOM APP

The *Unlock* Second Edition Classroom App ...

- offers extra, **motivating** practice in speaking, critical thinking and language
- provides a **convenient** bank of language and skills reference informed by our exclusive Corpus research ⊙
- is easily **accessible** and **navigable** from students' mobile phones
- is fully **integrated** into every unit
- provides Unlock-**specific** activities to extend the lesson whenever you see this symbol 📱

... so that students can easily get the right, extra practice they need, when they need it.

INSIGHT

The learning material on a Classroom app is most effective when it's an integral, well-timed part of a lesson.

CONTENT

Every unit of *Unlock* Second Edition is enhanced with bespoke Classroom app material to extend the skills and language students are learning in the book. The symbol 📱 shows when to use the app.

RESULTS

Students are motivated by having relevant extension material on their mobile phones to maximize their language learning. Teachers are reassured that the Classroom App adds real language-learning value to their lessons.

RESEARCH

We have gained deeper insights to inform *Unlock* Second Edition by ...

- carrying out **extensive market research** with teachers and students to fully understand their needs throughout the course's development
- consulting **academic research** into critical thinking
- refining our vocabulary syllabus using our **exclusive Corpus research** ⊙

... so that you can be assured of the quality of *Unlock* Second Edition.

INSIGHT

- Consultation with global Advisory Panel
- Comprehensive reviews of material
- Face-to-face interviews and Skype™ calls
- Classroom observations

CONTENT

- Improved critical thinking
- 100% new video and video lessons
- Clearer contexts for language presentation and practice
- Text-by-text glossaries
- Online Workbooks with more robust content
- Comprehensive teacher support

RESULTS

"Thank you for all the effort you've put into developing Unlock Second Edition. As far as I can see, I think the new edition is more academic and more appealing to young adults."

Burçin Gönülsen,
Işık Üniversity, Turkey

Unlock your knowledge

Encourages discussion around the themes of the unit with inspiration from interesting questions and striking images.

Watch and listen

Features an engaging and motivating video which generates interest in the topic and develops listening skills.

LISTENING

Listening 1

Provides information about the topic and practises pre-listening, while-listening and post-listening skills. This section may also include a focus on pronunciation which will further enhance listening comprehension.

Language development

Practises the vocabulary and grammar from Listening 1 and pre-teaches the vocabulary and grammar for Listening 2.

Listening 2

Presents a second listening text on the topic, often in a different format, and serves as a model for the speaking task.

SPEAKING

Critical thinking

Develops the lower- and higher-order thinking skills required for the speaking task.

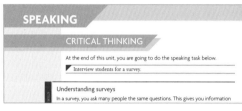

Preparation for speaking

Presents and practises functional language, pronunciation and speaking strategies for the speaking task.

Speaking task

Uses the skills and language learned throughout the unit to support students in producing a presentational or interactional speaking task. This is the unit's main learning objective.

Objectives review

Allows learners to evaluate how well they have mastered the skills covered in the unit.

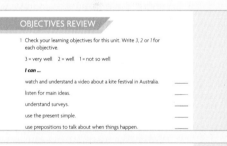

Wordlist

Lists the key vocabulary from the unit. The most frequent words used at this level in an academic context are highlighted.

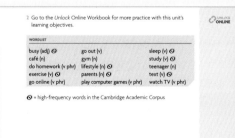

Unlock offers 56 hours per Student's Book, which is extendable to 90 hours with the Classroom App, Online Workbook and other additional activities in the Teacher's Manual and Development Pack.

Unlock is a paired-skills course with two separate Student's Books per level. For levels 1–5 (CEFR A1 – C1), these are **Reading, Writing and Critical Thinking** and **Listening, Speaking and Critical Thinking**. They share the same unit topics so you have access to a wide range of material at each level. Each Student's Book provides access to the Classroom App and Online Workbook.

Unlock Basic has been developed for pre-A1 learners. **Unlock Basic Skills** integrates reading, writing, listening, speaking and critical thinking in one book to provide students with an effective and manageable learning experience. **Unlock Basic Literacy** develops and builds confidence in literacy. The *Basic* books also share the same unit topics and so can be used together or separately, and **Unlock Basic Literacy** can be used for self-study.

Student components

Resource	Description	Access

Student's Books	• Levels 1–5 come with Classroom App, Online Workbook, and downloadable audio and video
	
	    – Levels 1–4 (8 units)
	
	    – Level 5 (10 units)
	
	• *Unlock Basic Skills* comes with downloadable audio and video (11 units)
	
	• *Unlock Basic Literacy* comes with downloadable audio (11 units)
		• The Classroom App and Online Workbook are on the **CLMS** and are accessed via the unique code inside the front cover of the Student's Book
		
		• The audio and video are downloadable from the Resources tab on the **CLMS**

Online Workbook	• Levels 1–5 only • Extension activities to further practise the language and skills learned • All-new vocabulary activities in the Online Workbooks practise the target vocabulary in new contexts	• The Online Workbook is on the **CLMS** and is accessed via the unique code inside the front cover of the Student's Book
Classroom App	• Levels 1–5 only • Extra practice in speaking, critical thinking and language	• The app is downloadable from the **Apple App Store** or **Google Play** • Students use the same login details as for the **CLMS**, and then they are logged in for a year
Video	• Levels 1–5 and *Unlock Basic Skills* only • All the video from the course	• The video is downloadable from the Resources tab on the **CLMS**
Audio	• All the audio from the course	• The audio is downloadable from the Resources tab on the **CLMS** and from **cambridge.org/unlock**

Teacher components

Resource	Description	Access
Teacher's Manual and Development Pack	• One manual covers Levels 1–5 • It contains flexible lesson plans, lesson objectives, additional activities and common learner errors as well as professional development for teachers, *Developing critical thinking skills in your students* • It comes with downloadable audio and video, vocabulary worksheets and peer-to-peer teacher training worksheets	• The audio, video and worksheets are downloadable from the Resources tab on the **CLMS** and from **eSource** via the code inside the front cover of the manual
Presentation Plus	• Software for interactive whiteboards so you can present the pages of the Student's Books and easily play audio and video, and check answers	• Please contact your sales rep for codes to download Presentation Plus from **eSource**

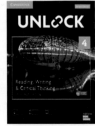

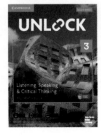

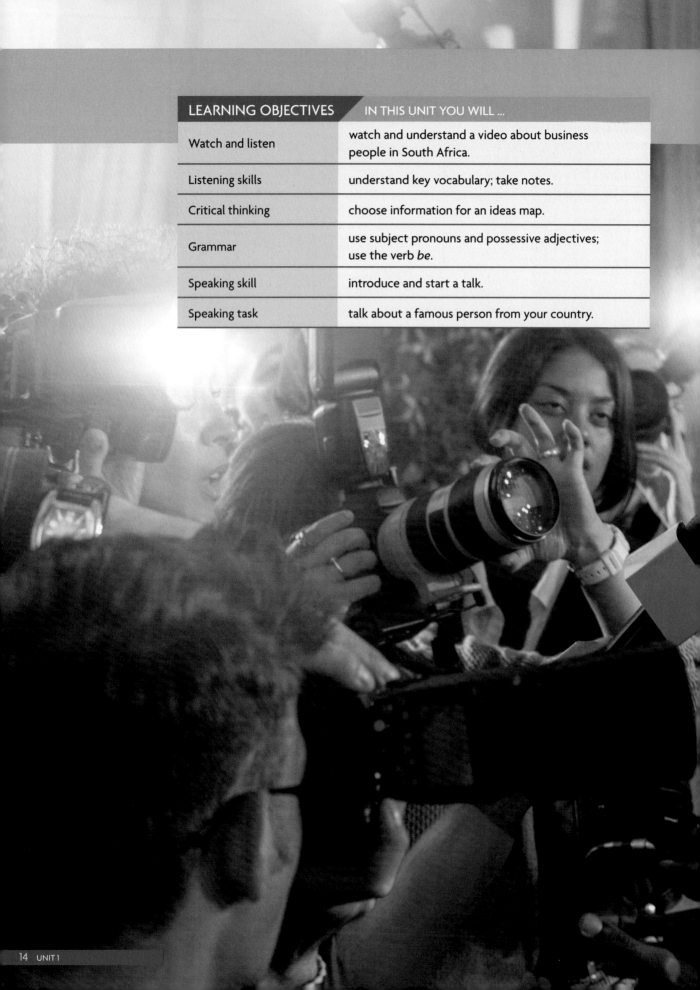

LEARNING OBJECTIVES	IN THIS UNIT YOU WILL …
Watch and listen	watch and understand a video about business people in South Africa.
Listening skills	understand key vocabulary; take notes.
Critical thinking	choose information for an ideas map.
Grammar	use subject pronouns and possessive adjectives; use the verb *be*.
Speaking skill	introduce and start a talk.
Speaking task	talk about a famous person from your country.

UNLOCK YOUR KNOWLEDGE

Work with a partner. Ask and answer the questions.

1 What can you see in the photo?
2 What is happening?
3 What do you think this person is saying?

PLUS

  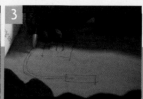 

PREPARING TO WATCH

1 Work with a partner and answer the questions.

   1 What clothes are you wearing today?

   2 Where do you buy most of your clothes? Where do they come from?

   3 Do you know someone who has his or her own business? What kind of business is it?

2 Look at the pictures from the video. Match the sentences (a–d) to the photos (1–4).

   a Soweto is in the South African city of Johannesburg.

   b The towers have colourful pictures.

   c The woman has her own clothing business.

   d The man is drawing a picture of a lamp.

GLOSSARY

design (v) to draw or plan something before you make it

sew (v) to make or repair clothing with a needle and thread

material (n) cloth for making clothes

business (n) a company

successful (adj) having a good result

equipment (n) tools or machines

WHILE WATCHING

3 ▶ Watch the video. Tick (✔) the information that you hear.

☐ 1 Mandisa Zwane has her own clothing business.
☐ 2 Mandisa Zwane's business is not very successful.
☐ 3 The Box Shop helps people in Soweto to start their own businesses.
☐ 4 The businesses in Soweto sell to shops in many countries.
☐ 5 Valaphi Mpolweni sells paintings and other art.
☐ 6 With help and advice from Box Shop, many small businesses in Soweto are growing.

UNDERSTANDING DETAIL

4 ▶ Watch again. Circle the correct word.

1 Mandisa Zwane *sews / buys* clothes in Soweto.
2 She uses *expensive / colourful* African material.
3 *Four / Ten* other people work for Zwane.
4 The Box Shop gives business owners *money / advice*.
5 Valaphi Mpolweni sells furniture to shops in *the United States / Africa*.

5 Complete the sentences with words from the box.

MAKING INFERENCES

business	popular	difficult	workers

1 Mandisa needed more _____ because her business is very successful.
2 It is probably _____ to start your own business in Soweto.
3 The people at the Box Shop have a good knowledge of _____ .
4 Mpolweni's furniture is _____ in the United States.

DISCUSSION

6 Work with a partner and answer the questions.

1 Do you like the clothing that Mandisa Zwane makes? Why / Why not?
2 Do you want to have your own business? Why / Why not?
3 Do you think it is difficult to have your own business? Why / Why not?

LISTENING

LISTENING 1

PREPARING TO LISTEN

1 Talk with a partner. When you meet people for the first time, what do you tell them about yourself?

- your name?
- your last name?
- your family?
- your job?

Understanding key vocabulary

Before you listen, try to understand the key vocabulary in the Preparing to listen exercises. These words will help you understand the main ideas of the listening.

2 You are going to listen to three students talking about themselves. Before you listen, read about two other students. Then write the words in bold from the texts in the table below.

My name's Fahd and I'm from Saudi Arabia. I'm 19 and I'm a **student**. I have a **brother** and three **sisters**. My **family**'s from Riyadh, but my brother has a house in Jeddah. He's a **doctor** there.

My name's Li Yu Lin and I'm from China. I'm 21 and I'm a student. I have one brother. He is an **engineer**. We have a hotel in Shanghai. My **mother** and **father** are the **managers**.

topic	key vocabulary
family	brother,
jobs	doctor,

PRONUNCIATION FOR LISTENING

Syllable stress

When a word has more than one syllable, one syllable in the word has more stress than the others. You say it in a longer, louder way than the other syllables. The stressed syllables in these words are underlined.

<u>bro</u>-ther   man-a-<u>ger</u>   <u>sis</u>-ter

3 🔊 1.1 How many syllables do these words have? Listen and write *1, 2* or *3*.

_____ **1** introduce	_____ **5** twenty	_____ **9** computer	
_____ **2** please	_____ **6** eighteen	_____ **10** college	
_____ **3** Peru	_____ **7** study		
_____ **4** Turkey	_____ **8** business		

4 🔊 1.1 Listen again. Underline the stressed syllables in Exercise 3.

WHILE LISTENING

5 🔊 1.2 Listen to the three students. Match the countries to the students.

Peru Japan Turkey

LISTENING FOR
MAIN IDEAS

1 Nehir _____

2 Carlos _____

3 Koko _____

6 🔊 1.2 Listen again. Choose the correct answers.

1 The students talk about ...
   a teachers in their school.   c their friends at home.
   b students in their class.

2 They tell us about their ...
   a families.   c homes.
   b holidays.

3 They also tell us what they want to ...
   a do on holiday.   c study at university.
   b do at home.

LISTENING
FOR DETAIL

7 🔊 1.2 Write T (true) or F (false) next to the sentences. Correct the
false sentences. Then listen again and check your answers.

_____ 1 Koko's a student.   _____ 4 Nehir has a sister.
_____ 2 Koko is 18.   _____ 5 Carlos's father is a doctor.
_____ 3 Nehir is 19.   _____ 6 Carlos wants to study
                                              Business.

8 Work with a partner. Ask and answer questions about the students in
Exercise 5. Take notes in the table.

1 What's his / her name?
2 How old is he / she?
3 Where's he / she from?
4 Does he / she have any brothers or sisters?
5 What does he / she want to do in the future?

	1 What's his / her name?	2 How old is he / she?	3 Where's he / she from?	4 Does he / she have any brothers or sisters?	5 What does he / she want to do in the future?
student 1	Nehir				
student 2					
student 3					

DISCUSSION

9 Work with a partner. Talk about the things below.

- your name (*I'm ...*)
- what you do (*I'm ...*)
- your country and hometown (*I'm from ...*)
- people in your family (*I have ...* , *My father's a ...* , *My mother's a ...*)
- your plans for the future (*I want to ...*)

10 Work with a new partner. Talk about your partner in Exercise 9.

I'm going to tell you about [Paolo]. He's / She's [18]. He's / She's from [Brazil]. He's / She's from [Recife]. He's / She's a [student]. He / She has [two sisters]. He / She wants to [study Business].

SUBJECT PRONOUNS AND POSSESSIVE ADJECTIVES

GRAMMAR

subject pronouns	possessive adjectives
I	my
you	your
he	his
she	her
it	its
we	our
they	their

Use subject pronouns before a verb.

I'm Carlos.

She's a student in our class.

He wants to study Business.

Use possessive adjectives before a noun.

My family's from Bogotá.

Her mother's from Sapporo.

His father's from Al-Ain.

1 Look at the underlined word(s). Write the correct subject pronouns in the gaps to replace the underlined words.

   1 My sister is a doctor. _____ works in a hospital.
   2 My parents work in a hotel. _____ 're managers.
   3 My name is Koko. _____ 'm a student.
   4 Where is Recife? _____ 's in Brazil.
   5 Reina and Mari are both from Canada. _____ 're from Toronto.
   6 My brother and I are students. _____ 're in two classes together.

2 Write the correct possessive adjectives in the gaps.

   1 This is Koko's book. → This is _____her_____ book.
   2 This is my brother's car. → This is _____ car.
   3 This is our daughter's school. → This is _____ school.
   4 This is Pedro and Isobel's house. → This is _____ house.
   5 This is my town and my family's town. → This is _____ town.

3 Circle the correct answers.

1 *She / Her* name's Kerry.
2 Is this *you / your* house?
3 This bag is nice. Is it *you / your* bag?
4 *He / His* is the manager of a shop.
5 *They / Their* teacher is from Egypt.

6 I'd like to study at this university. *It / Its* courses are very good.
7 *I / My* have a problem with *I / my* computer.
8 *We / Our* have a restaurant in *we / our* hotel.

PLUS

THE VERB *BE*

The verb *be* has three present forms: *am* (*'m*), *is* (*'s*) and *are* (*'re*).

subject	*be*	
I	am	
You / We / They	are	from London.
He / She / It	is	

contractions:	
singular	plural
I **am** → I'm	We **are** → We're
You **are** → You're	You **are** → You're
He **is** / She **is** / It **is** → He's / She's / It's	They **are** → They're

It is normal to use contractions in conversation.

I'm from the UK.   It's a photo of my friend.   They're from London.

Add *not* to make the negative.

singular			plural		
subject	*be + not*		subject	*be + not*	
I	am **not**		You		
You	are **not**	a student.	We	are **not**	Australian.
He / She / It	is **not**		They		

negative contractions	
singular	plural
I am not → I'm **not**	You are not → You're **not** / You **aren't**
You are not → You're **not** / You **aren't**	We are not → We're **not** / We **aren't**
He is not → He's **not** / He **isn't**	They are not → They're **not** / They **aren't**
She is not → She's **not** / She **isn't**	
It is not → It's **not** / It **isn't**	

The verb is before the subject in questions.

Is <u>she</u> from Turkey? **Are** <u>you</u> from Istanbul? **What's** <u>her name</u>?

4 🔊 1.3 Listen and circle the forms you hear.

A

Kerry: (1) *Who's / Who is* your best friend, Yasemin?

Yasemin: Her (2) *name's / name is* Meral.

Kerry: How (3) *old is / old's* she?

Yasemin: She's 20.

Kerry: Is she from Turkey?

Yasemin: Yes, but she (4) *is not / isn't* from Ankara like me. (5) *She is / She's* from İzmir.

B

Kayo: Excuse me, Kerry. Are you from Sydney?

Kerry: No, no, (6) *I am not / I'm not* from Australia. (7) *I am / I'm* from England. But my grandparents are Australian. They (8) *are not / 're not* from Sydney. (9) *They are / They're* from Melbourne.

Kayo: Are your parents English?

Kerry: Yes – and my sisters. (10) *We are / We're* all English.

5 Write the correct form of *be* in the gaps in the dialogue. Add *not* if necessary.

A: (1) _____Is_____ your school in Cairo?

B: No, it (2) _____ . It (3) _____ in Abu Dhabi in the UAE.

A: (4) _____ you from there?

B: Yes, I (5) _____ .

A: What do you study?

B: Business.

A: (6) _____ your parents in business?

B: No, they (7) _____ . My mother (8) _____ a doctor and my father (9) _____ a teacher.

A: Do you have brothers and sisters?

B: Yes. I have two brothers.

A: (10) _____ they students?

B: Yes. We (11) _____ all students at the same university.

PLUS

6 Work with a partner. Practise the dialogue. Give answers which are true for you.

PREPARING TO LISTEN

1 What do you think is the best job in the world? What do you think is the worst? Compare with a partner. Does he or she agree?

2 You are going to listen to two students talking about a famous person (someone many people know) from their country. Before you listen, look at the photos. Write the people's jobs below. Use the jobs in the vocabulary box to help you. More than one job is possible.

USING YOUR
KNOWLEDGE

UNDERSTANDING
KEY VOCABULARY

> **businessman** (n)   **businesswoman** (n)
> **chef** (n)   **scientist** (n)   **teacher** (n)   **writer** (n)

a Nadiya Hussain writes about food.

_____

b Salman Khan – Education for all

_____

c Larry Page – Co-founder of Google

_____

d Ursula Burns – former CEO of Xerox

_____

e Bill Nye – The Science Guy

_____

f Jamie Oliver cooking

_____

PLUS

3 Discuss in pairs. Which of the jobs from Exercise 2 do you want to do? Why?

4 🔊 1.4 Listen to the words for jobs in Exercise 2. Write the number of syllables in each word next to it. Then listen again and underline the stressed syllables.

1 writer _____
2 teacher _____
3 businessman _____

4 businesswoman _____
5 chef _____
6 scientist _____

LISTENING FOR
MAIN IDEAS

WHILE LISTENING

GLOSSARY

creative (adj) good at thinking of new ideas or using imagination

free (adj) not costing any money

5 🔊 1.5 Listen to two students, Marie and Clare, talking about two famous people from their countries. The people are in the photos in Exercise 2. Answer the questions.

1 Which person does Marie talk about? _____
2 What jobs does Marie's person have? _____
3 Which person does Clare talk about? _____
4 What jobs does Clare's person have? _____

SKILLS

Taking notes

When you listen to a presentation or talk, it's a good idea to take notes. This helps you remember the information later. When you take notes, you write down the important information you hear. You do not need to write complete sentences.

6 🔊 1.5 Listen again and take notes.

Nadiya Hussain: family _____

_____

famous for _____

_____

other information _____

_____

Salman Khan: family _____

_____

famous for _____

_____

other information _____

_____

7 🔊 1.5 Match the start of the sentences (1–8) to the endings (a–h). Use your notes from Exercise 6 to help you. Then listen again and check your answers.

1 Nadiya's husband is
2 Nadiya is very
3 Nadiya is a writer,
4 Salman's mother is
5 Salman has
6 Nadiya and her husband have
7 Salman is
8 Salman's wife is

a two sons and a daughter.
b a doctor.
c a manager.
d creative.
e a chef and a TV presenter.
f from India.
g a son and a daughter.
h from California.

DISCUSSION

8 Work with a partner.

Student A: Go to page 192.
Student B: Go to page 194.

SPEAKING

CRITICAL THINKING

At the end of this unit, you are going to do the speaking task below.

▸ Tell your group about a famous person from your country.

Choosing information for an ideas map

An *ideas map* helps you think about the topic and organize information about it. It also helps you to remember key information and vocabulary. Choose one main topic and 3–4 key words for your ideas map.

 UNDERSTAND

1 Look at the ideas map below and answer the questions.

  1 What is the main topic of the map?
  2 What are the three other topics in the map?

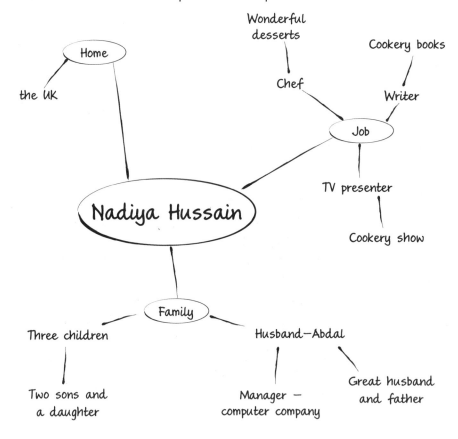

2 Write information about Salman Khan in the ideas map. Use your notes from Listening 2 to help you. Add more circles and lines for your information. Then check your ideas map with other students. Are there any differences?

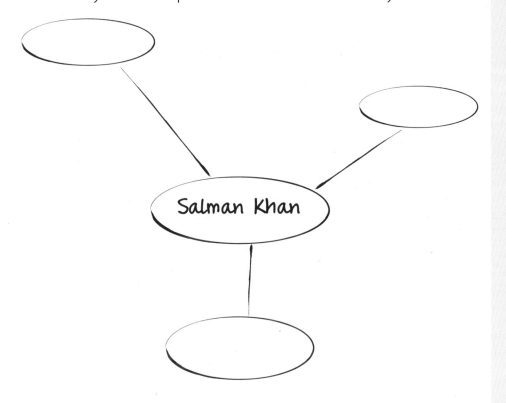

3 Work with a partner. Look at the ideas maps for Nadiya Hussain and Salman Khan. What do you remember about them? Take turns saying things about each person.

4 Make an ideas map for a famous person from your country.

  1 Think of an interesting famous person from your country.
  2 Write the name of the person in the centre.
  3 Find a photo and information about the person on the internet.
  4 Think about the person's country, job, family, home and why they are famous. Write 3–4 key words for these topics (for example, husband – *Abdal, writer, three children, creative*). Add them to your ideas map.

5 Work with a partner. Ask and answer questions about the people in your ideas map.

  • Who's the person in your ideas map?
  • Who is in his / her family?
  • Where's he / she from?
  • What is his / her job?
  • Why is he / she famous?

PREPARATION FOR SPEAKING

COUNTRIES AND NATIONALITIES

1 Work with a partner. Complete the table with words for nationalities.

Student A: Go to page 192.
Student B: Go to page 194.

name	country	nationality
Ana García	Mexico	Mexican
Eunseong Kim	South Korea	South Korean
Tim Berners-Lee	the UK	British
Karim Abdel Aziz	Egypt	(1)
Lin Dan	China	Chinese
Majid Al Futtaim	the UAE	(2)
Haruki Murakami	Japan	(3)
Zeynep Ahunbay	Turkey	(4)
Brandon Stanton	the United States	(5)
Fatma Al Nabhani	Oman	(6)

2 Write words from the table in the gaps.

1 Eunseong Kim is a famous _____ scientist.
2 Ana García is from _____ .
3 Karim Abdel Aziz is an _____ actor.
4 Haruki Murakami is from _____ .
5 Lin Dan is a famous _____ badminton player.
6 Brandon Stanton is a famous _____ photographer.
7 Fatma Al Nabhani is a famous _____ tennis player.
8 Majid Al Futtaim is a famous _____ businessman.

VOCABULARY FOR JOBS

3 Work in pairs. Look at the words for jobs. Add the missing job words to complete the table.

PLUS

verb + -er/-r	verb + -or	noun + -er	noun + -ist
write: writer	act: actor	football: footballer	art: artist
dance: _____	direct: _____	garden: _____	journal: _____
sing: _____		photograph: _____	
paint: _____		drive: _____	
manage: _____		engine: _____	
play: _____		design: _____	
present: _____			
teach: _____			

INTRODUCING AND STARTING A TALK

4 🔊 1.6 Choose the correct phrases. Then listen and check.

1 _____ about a famous person from Mexico.
   a I'm going to tell for you
   b I'm going to tell you
   c I'm going to tell

2 Ana García is _____ .
   a famous Mexican chef
   b a famous Mexican chef
   c the famous Mexican chef

3 _____ Haruki Murakami.
   a It has
   b This has
   c This is

4 _____ a famous Japanese writer.
   a His is
   b It is
   c He's

PRONUNCIATION FOR SPEAKING

Saying words and sentences in syllables

To help say a word or sentence, start with the last syllable. This helps us put the stress in the correct place.

er　　　　　　　　ball-er　　　　　　　　foot-ball-er

We do the same with sentences to show the important words.

5 🔊 1.7 Listen, read and repeat.

- er　　　　　　　sign-er　　　　　　　　　de-<u>sign</u>-er
- mous de-<u>sign</u>-er　　　fa-mous de-<u>sign</u>-er
- a <u>fa</u>-mous de-<u>sign</u>-er　　she's a <u>fam</u>-ous de-<u>sign</u>-er

6 🔊 1.8 Listen and repeat.

1　I'm <u>going</u> to <u>tell</u> you about two <u>famous</u> <u>people</u> from <u>Egypt</u>.
2　Karim Abdel Aziz is a famous actor.
3　Carmen Suleiman's a famous singer.
4　Karim's father is Mohammed Abdel Aziz.
5　He's a film director.
6　Karim's aunt is Samira Muhsin.
7　She's an actor.

7 🔊 1.8 Underline the stressed syllables in the sentences in Exercise 6. Then listen and repeat again.

8　Change the sentences in Exercise 6 so they are true about people from your country.

I'm going to tell you about two famous people from China.

Lin Dan's a famous badminton player.

9　Practise saying your sentences.

SPEAKING TASK

Tell your group about a famous person from your country.

PREPARE

1 Look back at the ideas map you created in the Critical thinking section, in Exercise 4. Review your notes and add any new information you want to include in your presentation. In your talk you will:

- introduce your person.
- show your photo.
- talk about your person's job, family and home.
- Talk about why your person is famous.

2 Prepare an introduction for your talk.

3 Read the Task checklist as you prepare your talk.

TASK CHECKLIST	✔
Use an ideas map.	
Talk about a famous person from your country.	
Use the verb *be*, possessive adjectives and subject pronouns correctly.	
Use syllable stress correctly.	

PRACTISE

4 Practise giving your talk with a partner. Listen to your partner's talk and ask questions.

PRESENT

5 Work in small groups. Talk about the famous person from your country. Show people in your group your photo. When you listen to other students, take notes in the table about each person.

	person 1	person 2	person 3	person 4
name				
country				
job				
family				
home				
famous for				

6 Talk in your group. Which person do you want to meet? Why? Tell the class.

OBJECTIVES REVIEW

1 Check your learning objectives for this unit. Write *3, 2* or *1* for each objective.

3 = very well   2 = well   1 = not so well

I can ...

watch and understand a video about business people in South Africa.   _____

understand key vocabulary.   _____

take notes.   _____

choose information for an ideas map.   _____

use subject pronouns and possessive adjectives.   _____

use the verb *be*.   _____

introduce and start a talk.   _____

talk about a famous person from my country.   _____

2 Go to the *Unlock* Online Workbook for more practice with this unit's learning objectives.

WORDLIST		
brother (n) ⊙	engineer (n) ⊙	scientist (n) ⊙
businessman (n)	family (n) ⊙	sister (n) ⊙
businesswoman (n)	father (n) ⊙	student (n) ⊙
chef (n)	free (adj) ⊙	teacher (n) ⊙
creative (adj) ⊙	manager (n) ⊙	writer (n) ⊙
doctor (n) ⊙	mother (n) ⊙	

⊙ = high-frequency words in the Cambridge Academic Corpus

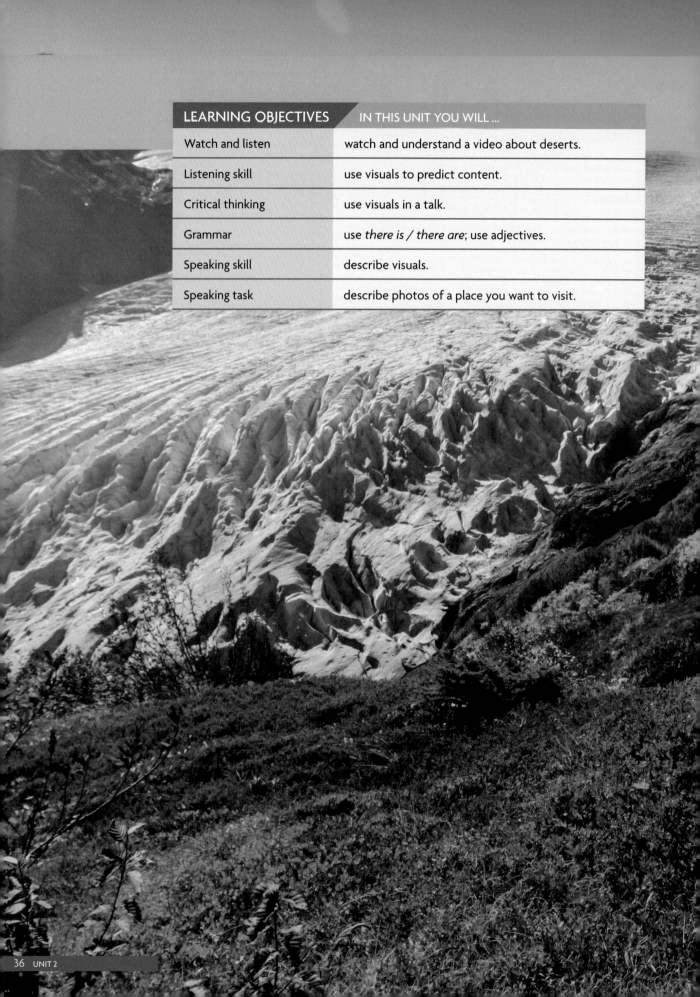

LEARNING OBJECTIVES	IN THIS UNIT YOU WILL ...
Watch and listen	watch and understand a video about deserts.
Listening skill	use visuals to predict content.
Critical thinking	use visuals in a talk.
Grammar	use *there is / there are*; use adjectives.
Speaking skill	describe visuals.
Speaking task	describe photos of a place you want to visit.

SEASONS

UNL**⌬**CK YOUR KNOWLEDGE

Work with a partner. Ask and answer the questions.

1 What do you see in the photo?
2 What is unusual about this photo?
3 Do you like hot or cold weather?

  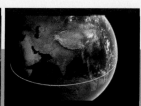 

PREPARING TO WATCH

ACTIVATING YOUR KNOWLEDGE

1 Work with a partner. Discuss the questions.

1 How many seasons are there in your country?
2 Does it rain often? When does it rain?
3 What are the most famous deserts in the world?
4 What is the weather in a desert like?

PREDICTING CONTENT USING VISUALS

2 Look at the photos from the video. Write *T* (true) or *F* (false) next to the statements. Correct the false statements.

_____ 1 A desert is dry.

_____

_____ 2 It does not rain often in a desert.

_____

_____ 3 There are several deserts on Earth.

_____

_____ 4 A desert is flat.

_____

GLOSSARY

climate (n) the weather of a particular place

equator (n) an imaginary line around the centre of the Earth

inch (n) a unit of measure, about 2.5 cm (centimetres)

spin (v) to turn round and round

WHILE WATCHING

UNDERSTANDING MAIN IDEAS

3 ▶ Watch the video. Circle the correct answers.

1 A desert is *very hot / not very hot* in the summer during the day.
2 A desert *has / does not have* a lot of water.
3 *There are / There are not* different plants in a desert.
4 Hot air comes from *near the equator / the desert*.

4 ▶ Watch again. Choose the correct answers.

1 The Sonoran Desert is in _____ .
   a North Africa
   b the Middle East
   c North America

2 In the summer, the temperature in the Sonoran Desert can reach _____ .
   a 122 °F (50 °C)
   b 22 °F (−5 °C)
   c 112 °F (44 °C)

3 There are more deserts like the Sonoran desert in _____ .
   a South America, Japan and North Africa
   b the Middle East, India and North Africa
   c Taiwan, India and North Africa

5 Write the words from the box in the gaps.

| careful   difficult   fruits and vegetables   rain |

1 It is _____ to live in a desert.
2 There is little _____ in a desert.
3 Many _____ do not grow in a desert.
4 People need to be _____ in a desert.

DISCUSSION

6 Work with a partner. Discuss the questions.

1 Is there a desert in your country? What is the desert's name?
2 How is the climate different in a desert?
3 Do you want to live in or near a desert? Why / Why not?

LISTENING

PREPARING TO LISTEN

UNDERSTANDING
KEY VOCABULARY

1 You are going to listen to a talk about different seasons. Before you listen, use the words in the box to complete the sentences below.

> **cold** (adj) having a low temperature
> **autumn** (n) the season of the year between summer and winter
> **hot** (adj) having a high temperature
> **snow** (n) soft, white pieces of frozen water which fall from the sky
> **spring** (n) the season of the year between winter and summer
> **temperature** (n) how hot or cold something is
> **weather** (n) the temperature or conditions outside, for example, if it is hot, cold, sunny, etc.

1 The sun is very _____ .
2 Brrr! I'm _____ . I need my hat and jacket.
3 The _____ is beautiful! It's white and clean. This is my favourite kind of _____ .
4 _____ is between winter and summer.
5 It's _____ now. The trees are red and orange and it's almost winter.
6 The _____ is -34.4 °C (degrees Celsius). Let's stay inside.

2 Work with a partner. Discuss your answers.

USING YOUR
KNOWLEDGE

Describe the weather in your country.
What is your favourite season? Use the words in the box above to help you.

Predicting content using visuals

Visuals can be photos, pictures, graphs or tables. Use visuals to help you understand the topic and important ideas.

3 Look at the photos and answer the questions.

1 These photos are all from the same place. Do you want to visit this place? Why / Why not?

2 Which photo shows hot weather? _____

3 Which photo shows a beach (an area next to water with sand or small stones where people like to sit)? _____

4 Which photo shows cold weather? _____

5 What season can you see in each photo? _____

6 What's the temperature outside in each photo? _____

PRONUNCIATION FOR LISTENING

SKILLS

Sentence stress

We stress important words in a sentence. Important words can be:

- nouns: *Dubai, July, Canada, lot, snow, winter, places*
- adjectives: *hot, sunny, cold*
- verbs: (but not *be*): *has, get*

Dubai's (hot) in July.
Canada has a lot of snow in winter.
We get snow when it's (cold) here.

4 🔊 2.1 Listen to the sentences and ...

- underline the nouns.
- circle the adjectives.
- highlight the verbs (but not *be*).

1 Take a look at the photos.
2 They are all from one place.
3 There's a beautiful beach next to a big lake.
4 It's winter and there's a mountain.
5 It's hot and there's sand.

WHILE LISTENING

LISTENING FOR
MAIN IDEAS

LISTENING
FOR DETAIL

5 🔊 2.2 Listen to a talk about a place with four seasons. Look at the photos in Exercise 3. Which photos does the teacher talk about?

6 🔊 2.2 Listen again. Write the missing words in the gaps.

1 It's a _____ day in summer.
2 There's lots of _____ .
3 It's also very _____ .
4 You can see it's _____ .
5 The temperature is a little cold and the trees change colour to _____ and _____ .
6 After the cold weather, _____ is welcome in Hokkaido.
7 The weather is _____ , so the flowers grow.

7 🔊 2.2 Listen again and check your answers.

DISCUSSION

8 Work in groups.

1 Choose a photo, but do not say which one.
2 Take turns talking about your photo. Use the phrases in the box.
3 Listen to the other students and guess the photo.

> Take a look at this photo. What can we see?
> It's ... hot, cold.
> This season is ... summer, winter, autumn, spring.
> There's a ... beach, lake.
> There's ... snow.

SEASONS

1 🔊 2.3 Listen and write the seasons from the box in the gaps (1–6).

> autumn   spring   summer   winter
> the dry season   the rainy season

1 Canada gets a lot of snow in _____ .

2 _____ in Washington, DC begins in June. It gets very hot.

3 _____ in London is from March to May. There are a lot of beautiful flowers.

4 In _____ , the trees change colour from green to orange or red.

5 In Korea, Japan and China, _____ begins in June and ends in July. It gets very wet.

6 _____ in Brazil begins in May. There is not a lot of rain.

2 Write countries or cities in the gaps (1–5). Then work in pairs. Read your sentences to your partner.

1 In _____ winters are very cold.
2 There is a rainy season in _____ .
3 _____ is very hot in the summer.
4 There is a dry season in _____ .
5 In _____ , there is a lot of rain in the spring.

WEATHER

3 Match the pictures (1–6) to the words for weather in the table.

picture	noun	adjective
	sun	sunny
	snow	snowy
	wind	windy
	rain	rainy
	cloud	cloudy
	storm	stormy

4 Circle the correct word.

1 I'm happy when it's *sun / sunny*.
2 There's a big, black *cloud / cloudy* in the sky.
3 I have a hat for when it's *rain / rainy*.
4 We get a lot of *storms / stormy* in April.
5 There's a lot of *snow / snowy* here in winter.
6 It's very *wind / windy* today!

5 Are the sentences in Exercise 4 true for you? Discuss your answers with a partner.

6 Complete the sentences about the weather in your city. Use words from the table in Exercise 3. Then work in pairs. Read your sentences to a partner.

1 It's _____ today.
2 There's a lot of _____ in spring.
3 In summer, it's _____ .
4 It's _____ in autumn.
5 In winter, it's _____ .

COLOURS

7 Write the correct number (1–7) next to the colours.

orange _____   yellow _____
red _____   blue _____
green _____   black _____
white _____

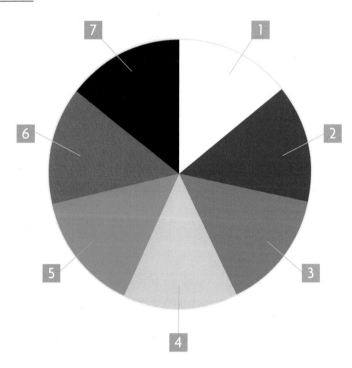

8 Work with a partner. Ask and answer the questions in the box about the words and phrases below.

> What colour is ... ?   It's ... / It can be ... or ...
> What colour are ... ?   They're ... / They can be ... or ...

1 water   3 trees   5 clouds
2 snow   4 sand   6 your family's car

PLUS

THERE IS / THERE ARE

You can use *There is* (*There's*) / *There are* to talk about people, places and things. Use *There is* with singular countable nouns and uncountable nouns. Use *There are* with plural countable nouns.

Countable nouns are things you can count. Use the singular or the plural form.
There is **a tree**. There are **four trees**.
Uncountable nouns are things you can't count.
There is **snow**. There is **rain**.

singular	plural
There is / There's a beach next to the lake.	**There are** people on the beach.
There is / There's snow on that mountain.	**There are** many trees in Hokkaido.

9 Are the nouns in the box countable or uncountable? Write them in the correct place in the table.

> cloud   river   rock   sand
> temperature   town   water   wind

countable nouns	uncountable nouns

10 Write the phrases from the box in the correct gap in the sentences. Use the nouns in the box in Exercise 9 to help you.

> There's a   There's   There are

1 _____ river in the photo.
2 _____ water in the lake.
3 _____ rocks on the beach.
4 _____ a lot of wind in April.
5 _____ small town in the mountains.
6 _____ black clouds in the sky.
7 _____ extreme temperatures in the winter.
8 _____ white sand on the beach.

11 🔊 2.4 Listen and check your answers. Then listen again and repeat.

PREPARING TO LISTEN

PREDICTING
CONTENT USING
VISUALS

1 You are going to listen to two students describe places. Before you listen, look at the photos and answer the questions.

1 What season is it in each photo?
2 Describe the weather.
3 What colours can you see?

UNDERSTANDING
KEY VOCABULARY

2 Work with a partner. Match the words from the box to numbers 1–7 in the photos.

> **desert** (n) a large, hot, dry area with very few plants _____
> **forest** (n) a large area of trees growing closely together _____
> **island** (n) an area of land which has water around it _____
> **mountain** (n) a very high hill _____
> **park** (n) a large area of grass and trees, usually very beautiful and everybody can use it _____
> **sea** (n) a large area of salt water _____
> **sky** (n) the area above the Earth where you can see clouds and the sun _____

PLUS

WHILE LISTENING

3 🔊 2.5 Listen to two students, Daniela and Altan, describing one of the places from Exercise 2.

1 Which photo does Daniela describe? _____
2 Which photo does Altan describe? _____
3 Which photos don't they describe? _____

LISTENING FOR MAIN IDEAS

4 🔊 2.5 Listen again and circle the correct answers.

1 Daniela describes a place …
   a in *spring / summer*.
   b in *Italy / Turkey*.
   c with a *forest / beach*.
   d she thinks it is *beautiful / snowy*.
2 Altan describes a place …
   a in *his / another* country.
   b in *autumn / winter*.
   c on a *hot / cold* day.
   d with a famous *park / hill*.

LISTENING FOR DETAIL

5 🔊 2.5 Listen again. What colours do you hear? Complete the table.

	colour	describes …
Daniela		building
		sea and sky
Altan		trees

DISCUSSION

6 Think of Listening 1 and Listening 2 and discuss the questions in pairs.

1 Daniela describes a place. Which season does it match in Listening 1? How is it the same? How is it different?
2 Altan describes a place. Which season does it match in Listening 1? How is it the same? How is it different?
3 Do any seasons in your country have extreme temperatures? Which ones?

SYNTHESIZING

SPEAKING

CRITICAL THINKING

At the end of this unit, you are going to do the speaking task below.

▶ Describe photos of a place you want to visit.

 UNDERSTAND

1 Work with a partner. Look at the photo on pages 36–37. Answer the questions in the table.

questions	answers
1 What is the photo of?	
2 Which season can you see in the photo?	
3 What is the weather like in the photo?	
4 Which colours can you see in the photo?	
5 Is the photo interesting? Why / Why not?	
6 What key vocabulary do you need to talk about this photo?	

Using visuals in a talk

When you give a talk, use visuals (pictures, diagrams and graphs). Visuals help people understand the information. They also make your talk more interesting.

Choose visuals that

- are interesting.
- give information about your topic.

2 Answer the questions.

1 What place do you want to visit? (e.g. New York, the Sahara Desert, Italy)

2 In what seasons do you want to visit the place? (e.g. summer, winter, the rainy season)

3 Use your answers from Exercise 2 in an internet search. Use questions 1–6 in Exercise 1 to help you choose two good photos of the place you want to visit. Use photos of the same season.

4 Answer questions 1–6 in Exercise 1 for the photos you found. Take notes.

5 Work with a partner. Take turns to ask and answer the questions about your partner's photos. Use the phrases from the box to answer.

1 Where is it?

2 What season is it?

3 What is the weather like?

4 What can you see there?

| It's in _____ . (country) |
| It's _____ . (season) |
| It's _____ . (weather adjective) |
| You can see _____ . (place) |
| There's a / There's _____ . (noun) |
| There are _____ . (noun) |

PREPARATION FOR SPEAKING

GIVING A TALK

1 🔊 2.6 Listen and match the sentence halves.

a	Good morning,	my first photo.
b	I'm going to talk about	everybody.
c	OK, so here's	photo of the park.
d	Hello, everybody!	I'm Altan.
e	I'm from	two photos of a place in spring.
f	Here's my	first photo.
g	Here's another	Samsun. Samsun is in Turkey.

PRONUNCIATION FOR SPEAKING

SKILLS

Sentence stress

In a normal sentence, one or two words have more stress than the others. You say them in a longer, louder way than the other words.

2 🔊 2.6 Listen again. Underline the words with stress in Exercise 1.

3 🔊 2.6 Listen again and repeat. Say the underlined words louder.

SKILLS

Pauses

You can also use pauses in a talk to help your listeners understand you.

OK, // I'm going to talk about two countries. // Here's the first photo. //

4 🔊 2.7 Listen and read the audio script. Note where there is a pause between words by writing //.

OK, // so today I want to talk about a place with extreme temperatures. Take a look at the photos. What seasons do you see?

DESCRIBING VISUALS

5 Look at the photos on this page and on page 53. What can you see?

1

6 2.8 Match the phrases (1–6) and sentences (a–f) to make a talk. Then listen and check.

1 Hello, everybody!
2 Today
3 Here's my first photo.
4 Right, so where is this place?
5 Here's another photo of the mountain.
6 It's a beautiful place.

a It's in Japan. This is Mount Fuji.
b There's a path and you can see there are people there. There are a lot of white clouds below.
c I'm going to talk about two photos of a place in spring.
d I want to go there.
e You can see there's a big mountain. There's a lot of snow. And there are trees. The trees are orange and red.
f OK, so I'm Khaled. I'm from Port Said in Egypt.

7 Work with a partner. Take turns to describe the photos on this page and on page 52. Look at the text in Exercise 6. Make Khaled's talk true for you.

PLUS

ADJECTIVES

GRAMMAR

Use adjectives to describe age (*young, old*), size (*big, small*), nationality (*Turkish, Japanese*), colour (*red, green*) and quality (*hot, cold*).

Adjectives go after the verb *be* (*am / is / are*) or before a noun.

The mountains are (big.)
I'm **Turkish**. The weather is (cold.) It's (windy.)
It's a (beautiful) place. It's a (sunny) day.
There are (white) clouds in the sky.

You often stress adjectives.

8 Write the adjective in brackets in the correct place in the sentence.

1 There are _____ clouds _____ in the _____ sky. (white)
2 It's a _____ day _____ in winter. (snowy)
3 There are some _____ mountains _____ in _____ Switzerland. (big)
4 It's a _____ day _____ in spring _____ . (sunny)
5 The trees _____ are _____ in the _____ autumn. (orange and red)
6 It's a _____ beach _____ . (beautiful)

9 Correct the mistakes in the sentences.

1 It's sun in the photo.

_____

2 There are clouds white.

_____

3 There's a mountain big.

_____

4 The people happy.

_____

5 There's a forest green.

_____

6 It's a rain day.

_____

SPEAKING TASK

Describe photos of a place you want to visit.

PREPARE

1 Look back at your notes in the Critical thinking section. Review your notes and think of words and phrases to use in your talk. Write them down to help you with your talk.

2 Read the Task checklist as you prepare your talk.

TASK CHECKLIST	✔
Prepare an introduction.	
Find key vocabulary for the photos (what you can see in the photos, weather, season, etc.).	
Describe the photos of a place you want to visit.	
Use sentence stress correctly.	

3 Think of questions you can ask the other students using language you have seen in this unit.

> Can you see … ?　　Where is … ?　　What … ?

PRACTISE

4 Practise your talk with a partner. Give your partner feedback:

1 What did you like about their talk?

2 What can they do better next time?

PRESENT

5 Work in small groups.

1 Take turns to describe photos or pictures of a place you want to visit.
2 Listen to the other students in your group. Take notes in the table and ask questions.

	example	student 1	student 2
student's name	Khaled		
country	Japan		
place	mountain		
season	spring		
weather	sunny		
things in the photos	There is a mountain. There are trees. There are clouds.		

6 Show your notes to the other students in your group. Check your notes and correct any mistakes.

OBJECTIVES REVIEW

1 Check your learning objectives for this unit. Write *3, 2* or *1* for each objective.

3 = very well   2 = well   1 = not so well

I can ...

watch and understand a video about deserts. _____

use visuals to predict content. _____

use visuals in a talk. _____

use *there is / there are.* _____

use adjectives. _____

describe visuals. _____

describe photos of a place I want to visit. _____

2 Go to the *Unlock* Online Workbook for more practice with this unit's learning objectives.

UNL⊙CK
ONLINE

WORDLIST

autumn (n) ⊙	mountain (n) ⊙	summer (n) ⊙
black (adj) ⊙	orange (adj)	sun (n) ⊙
blue (adj) ⊙	park (n) ⊙	sunny (adj)
climate (n) ⊙	rain (n) ⊙	temperature (n) ⊙
cloud (n) ⊙	rainy (adj)	the dry season (phr)
cloudy (adj)	red (adj) ⊙	the rainy season (phr)
cold (adj) ⊙	sea (n) ⊙	weather (n) ⊙
desert (n) ⊙	sky (n)	white (adj) ⊙
equator (n)	snow (n)	wind (n) ⊙
forest (n) ⊙	snowy (adj)	windy (adj)
green (adj) ⊙	spin (v)	winter (n) ⊙
hot (adj) ⊙	spring (n) ⊙	yellow (adj) ⊙
inch (n)	storm (n)	
island (n) ⊙	stormy (adj)	

⊙ = high-frequency words in the Cambridge Academic Corpus

LEARNING OBJECTIVES	IN THIS UNIT YOU WILL ...
Watch and listen	watch and understand a video about a kite festival in Australia.
Listening skill	listen for main ideas.
Critical thinking	understand surveys.
Grammar	use the present simple.
Speaking skill	use prepositions to talk about when things happen.
Speaking task	interview students for a survey.

UNL🔓CK YOUR KNOWLEDGE

1 What can you see in the photograph?

2 Why is the man on the right doing two things at the same time?

3 Circle the phrases that are true for you.

- I use the internet or a smartphone every day.
- I talk to friends every day.
- I do two things at the same time every day.

WATCH AND LISTEN

PREPARING TO WATCH

ACTIVATING YOUR KNOWLEDGE

1 Work with a partner and answer the questions.

1 Do you enjoy the beach? What do you like to do there?
2 Where can people fly a kite near your home? A park? A beach? Do you fly a kite?
3 Does your city have a famous festival? Describe it.

PREDICTING CONTENT USING VISUALS

2 Look at the pictures from the video. Match the sentences (a–d) to the photos (1–4).

a On most days, the sky above Bondi Beach is empty.
b The kites are in many different shapes and sizes.
c People watch the kites fly high in the sky.
d Some visitors take photos at the Festival of the Winds.

GLOSSARY

festival (n) a special day (or days) when people celebrate with music, dancing or games

contest (n) a game you try to win

magnificent (adj) very good or very beautiful

traditional (adj) in the old way

diamond (n) a shape with four sides, often used for kites

WHILE WATCHING

UNDERSTANDING MAIN IDEAS

3 ▶ Watch the video. Tick (✔) the true statements.

☐ 1 Sydney, Australia has beautiful beaches.
☐ 2 People come to Bondi Beach every day to fly kites.
☐ 3 People from many different countries come for the Festival of the Winds.
☐ 4 The contests are for people with experience with kites.
☐ 5 Some of the kites are in the shape of animals.

4 ▶ Watch again. Circle the correct answers.

1 More than _____ people live in Sydney, Australia.
   a 5 million   b 7 million   c 10 million
2 _____ is Sydney's most famous building.
   a Bondi Beach   b The Art Museum   c The Opera House
3 The Festival of the Winds occurs _____ .
   a on Saturday   b every year   c once a month
4 The traditional shape for kites is a _____ .
   a diamond   b box   c fish
5 Most of the people at the Festival of Winds come to _____ .
   a fly kites   b watch   c surf

5 Match the sentence halves.

1 Bondi Beach   a there are no kites on
2 On most days   Bondi Beach.
3 At the Festival of the Winds,   b are not for beginners.
  some people   c is popular with tourists.
4 The contests   d fly a kite for the first time.

DISCUSSION

6 Work with a partner and answer the questions.

1 Do you want to go to the Festival of the Winds? Why / Why not?
2 What other things do you think visitors do at the Festival of the Winds?
3 Do you like going to festivals? Why? / Why not?

LISTENING

LISTENING 1

PREPARING TO LISTEN

USING YOUR
KNOWLEDGE

1 You are going to listen to a discussion about lifestyles. Before you listen, work with a partner. Discuss the questions.

1 Each week, how much time do you spend ...
   • with friends?   • on your smartphone?   • on your computer?

2 Do you think the time you spend on each activity is
   a too much?   b too little?   c the right amount?

UNDERSTANDING
KEY VOCABULARY

2 Match the photos (a–g) to the sentences (1–7).

1 I like to **play computer games**. They are fun and exciting. _____

2 I feel good and have more energy when I **exercise**. _____

3 I am very tired and need to rest. I'm going to **sleep** well tonight. _____

4 I **watch TV** on Thursday nights. My favourite show comes on at 7 pm. _____

5 I like to **go online** and shop. I don't like going to shops – it takes too long. _____

6 I need to **do homework** tonight. I don't have time before school tomorrow. _____

7 I like to **text** friends because it is quicker than email. _____

PRONUNCIATION FOR LISTENING

SKILLS

Intonation in questions and statements

Intonation is the way your voice goes up and down when you speak.

Your voice often goes up ↗ when you ask *yes / no* questions. Your voice often goes down ↘ when you ask *information* questions or make a statement.

A: What's your name? ↘   B: My name is Jennifer. ↘
A: Are you from London? ↗   B: No. I'm from Manchester. ↘

3 🔊 3.1 Listen to the dialogue from the Skills box above and repeat.

4 🔊 3.2 Look at the questions and statements. Will the intonation go up or down? Write ↗ or ↘ in the boxes. Then listen and check.

1 What do you want to watch on TV? ☐
2 How many hours do you sleep every night? ☐
3 Who's between the ages of 13 and 19? ☐
4 Do you play computer games? ☐
5 It's important for people to exercise. ☐
6 Do you text a lot? ☐

SKILLS

Listening for main ideas

If you listen for the main idea(s), you try to understand these questions:

- Where are the speakers? (e.g. a university, a hospital, a hotel)
- Who are the speakers and how do they know each other? (e.g. family, friends, teacher and students)
- Why are they speaking? (e.g. They need information., They want help., They want to teach something.)

GLOSSARY

lifestyle (n) the way that you live

teenager (n) someone who is between 13 and 19 years old

LISTENING FOR
MAIN IDEAS

5 🔊 3.3 Listen to a discussion. Put a tick (✔) next to the correct answers.

1 The discussion is …
  a in a supermarket. ☐
  b in a classroom. ☐
  c in a restaurant. ☐

2 The discussion is between a teacher and …
  a students who exercise. ☐
  b students who do homework. ☐
  c all students in the class. ☐

3 The discussion is about …
  a busy students. ☐
  b Saturday and Sunday. ☐
  c lifestyles. ☐

LISTENING
FOR DETAIL

6 🔊 3.3 Listen again. Write T (true) or F (false) next to the statements.
Correct the false statements.

_____ 1 It's the afternoon.

_____

_____ 2 The students are teenagers.

_____

_____ 3 Abdul sleeps ten hours every night.

_____

_____ 4 Madiha usually watches TV at night.

_____

_____ 5 Mimi watches TV or goes online on Saturday and Sunday.

_____

_____ 6 Sandra exercises.

_____

DISCUSSION

7 Work with a partner. Ask and answer the questions.

1 What healthy things do you do? Do you enjoy doing them?
2 Do young people often exercise in your culture?

THE PRESENT SIMPLE

Statements

Use the present simple to talk about routines – activities that you usually do. Use the infinitive with I / you / we / they. Add -s or -es to the verb after he / she / it.

I You We They	**go** to work at 8:30.	He She It	**goes** to work at 8:30.

For the negative, use I / you / we / they + do + not before the infinitive. Use he / she / it + does + not before the infinitive.

In conversation, you can use the contractions (short forms) *don't* (*do not*) or *doesn't* (*does not*) before the infinitive.

I You We They	**do not work** at weekends. **don't work** at weekends.	He She It	**does not** work at weekends. **doesn't work** at weekends.

Have is irregular:
I / You / We / They **have** a friend in London.
He / She / It **has** a friend in London.

1 Circle the correct form of the verb in the present simple.

1 Peter and Barbara *have / has* busy lifestyles.
2 Peter *get up / gets up* at 6:00 every morning and *go / goes* to university.
3 He *don't eat / doesn't eat* breakfast, but he *have / has* coffee before his lesson *start / starts*.
4 Barbara *don't go / doesn't go* to university.
5 She *work / works* in a shop.
6 Peter *take / takes* the bus, but Barbara *walk / walks* to work.
7 Sometimes, at night, they both *make / makes* dinner.
8 Then Peter usually *do / does* homework and Barbara *exercise / exercises*.
9 In his free time, Peter *play / plays* computer games and Barbara *go / goes* online.
10 At weekends, they *don't like / doesn't like* to study or work.

GRAMMAR

Questions

Use *do* or *does* with the infinitive to ask *yes / no* questions.

yes / no questions				short answers	
do / does	subject	infinitive		yes	no
Do	you	cook?		Yes, I do.	No, I don't.
Does	he	go	to the gym?	Yes, he **does**.	No, he **doesn't**.

Information questions begin with a *wh-* word. They ask for information and cannot be answered with *yes* or *no*.

information questions			
wh- word	*do / does*	subject	infinitive
Where	do	I / you /we / they	live? / work? / study?
Where	does	he / she / it	live? / work? / study?

Other *wh-* words are: *who, what, when* and *why*. You can also use *how* in the same way.

how	*do / does*	subject	infinitive
How many hours	do	I / you /we / they	sleep? / work?
How many hours	does	he / she / it	sleep? / work?

2 Put the words in order to make questions.

1 exercise / you / Do / ?

_____

2 you / homework / do / Do / ?

_____

3 do / Which / computer games / play / you / ?

_____

4 in the evening / Do / watch / TV / you / ?

_____

5 Who / at the weekend / do / text / you / ?

_____

6 do / live / Where / you / ?

_____

7 you / do / at university / What / study / ?

_____

3 Write *do*, *does*, *don't* or *doesn't* in the gaps in the conversations.

1 **A:** _____ they exercise at weekends?
   B: No, they _____ .

2 **A:** _____ she walk to work?
   B: Yes, she _____ .

3 **A:** _____ you play computer games?
   B: Yes, I _____ .

4 **A:** _____ he like to cook?
   B: No, he _____ .

4 Write the questions to complete the conversations.

1 **A:** _____
   B: They live in Madrid.

2 **A:** _____
   B: She studies Medicine.

3 **A:** _____
   B: I work at a bank.

4 **A:** _____
   B: He goes to bed at ten o'clock.

5 **A:** _____
   B: I study with my friends, Sabir and Antonio.

5 Correct the mistakes in the questions.

1 You cook food for your family?

   _____

2 You do homework?

   _____

3 What you do at home?

   _____

4 Where go you with friends?

   _____

5 What smartphone you like?

   _____

6 Work in small groups. Ask and answer the questions in Exercise 5.

PLUS

VERB COLLOCATIONS

A *collocation* is a group of words which often go together. A collocation can be:

- a verb + noun / noun phrase: *do homework, play computer games*
- a verb + prepositional phrase: *go to the gym, eat at home*
- a verb + adverb: *go online*

Using collocations makes your English sound more natural.

7 Write the verbs from the box in the gaps. Use Exercise 1 on page 66 to help you.

| get   go   ~~have~~   make   play   take   watch |

1 ___have___ a class / coffee
2 _____ breakfast / lunch / dinner
3 _____ football / computer games
4 _____ home / to work / to the gym
5 _____ up (in the morning)
6 _____ the bus
7 _____ TV / films / DVDs

8 Write the verbs from the box in the table.

cook do eat go have play watch

food	free time
• (1) _cook_ food for your family • **eat out** at restaurants • **have** coffee with friends • (2)_____ at home • (3)_____ dinner with friends • **make** lunch	• **go out** with friends • (4)_____ TV • **go** to the cinema • (5)_____ sports • **play** computer games • (6)_____ to the gym • **chat** online • (7)_____ homework

PLUS

9 Write questions to ask your partner in the present simple. Use some verb collocations. Ask your partner the questions and answer your partner's questions.

1 Do you _____ ?
2 Do you _____ ?
3 Do you _____ ?
4 Where _____ ?
5 When _____ ?
6 What _____ ?

10 Work with another partner. Tell your new partner three things about your partner from Exercise 9. Use the present simple.

LISTENING 2

PREPARING TO LISTEN

USING YOUR
KNOWLEDGE

1 You are going to listen to an interview. Before you listen, work with a partner. Discuss the questions about your country.

1 Do people talk to people they don't know on the street?
2 Do students usually live with their parents?
3 Do students have a lot of free time?

2 Write the words from the box in the correct gap in the sentences below.

UNDERSTANDING
KEY VOCABULARY

> **busy** (adj) if you are busy, you are doing a lot
> **café** (n) a small restaurant for tea, coffee and snacks
> **go out** (v) to spend time with friends outside your home
> **gym** (n) a place where you can go to exercise and get fit
> **parents** (n) your mother and father
> **study** (v) to learn about a particular subject, either in a school or university or by reading books

1 I have a test on Friday. I need to _____ on Thursday.
2 I like to exercise. I go to the _____ every day.
3 Alan and Kate both work, so they usually don't have time to make dinner. They _____ to a restaurant every night.
4 I have dinner with my _____ on Sundays. They miss me because I no longer live at home.
5 We go to a _____ and have coffee every week.
6 My life is very _____ . I almost don't have time to sleep.

PLUS

3 When you ask and answer questions, it's important to use polite (friendly) words. Circle the polite words and phrases.

  1 **A:** Excuse me. I'd like to ask you a question.
    B: Don't talk to me. Not now.
  2 **A:** Can I have a few minutes of your time?
    B: Sure. No problem.
  3 **A:** Sorry. Do you have a minute?
    B: No. I'm afraid I don't.

4 🔊 3.4 Listen to the dialogues. Practise with a partner.

WHILE LISTENING

LISTENING FOR
MAIN IDEAS

5 🔊 3.5 Listen to an interview and answer the questions.

  1 Where are the speakers?
    a in a university
    h in a café
    c on the street
  2 Who are the speakers?
    a two strangers
    b a teacher and a student
    c good friends
  3 What does April want to know about?
    a lifestyles
    b computer games
    c gyms

6 🔊 3.5 Listen again. Write Jumana's answers in the questionnaire.

QUESTIONNAIRE

Name: Jumana   **Job:** university student

A   Home / Family

A1   Do you live with your parents?   Y ◯   N ◯

B   Work / Studies

B1   Do you work or study?   work ◯   study ◯

B2   What's your job? / What do you study?   Biology

C   Lifestyle

C1   Do you have a busy lifestyle?   Y ◯   N ◯

C2a   How do you relax?

C2b   Do you like to exercise?   Y ◯   N ◯

C2c   Do you go to a gym?   Y ◯   N ◯

C2d   Do you go to the cinema?   Y ◯   N ◯

C3a   When do you go out with friends?

C3b   Where do you go with your friends?

DISCUSSION

7   Work with a partner. Think of Listening 1 and Listening 2 and answer the questions.

1   In Listening 1, what things do the students do?
2   In Listening 2, what things does Jumana do?
3   Who has a busier lifestyle, the students or Jumana? Explain your answer.
4   Is your lifestyle more like the students' or Jumana's? How?

SPEAKING

CRITICAL THINKING

At the end of this unit, you are going to do the speaking task below.

Interview students for a survey.

SKILLS

Understanding surveys

In a survey, you ask many people the same questions. This gives you information about what most people think or do. For example, you can ask questions to learn about the lifestyles of students in your school or university.

APPLY

1 Before you write your survey, think of the information April asks about in her survey in Listening 2. Complete the ideas map below. Write the topics from her questionnaire on page 73 and the information from her questions.

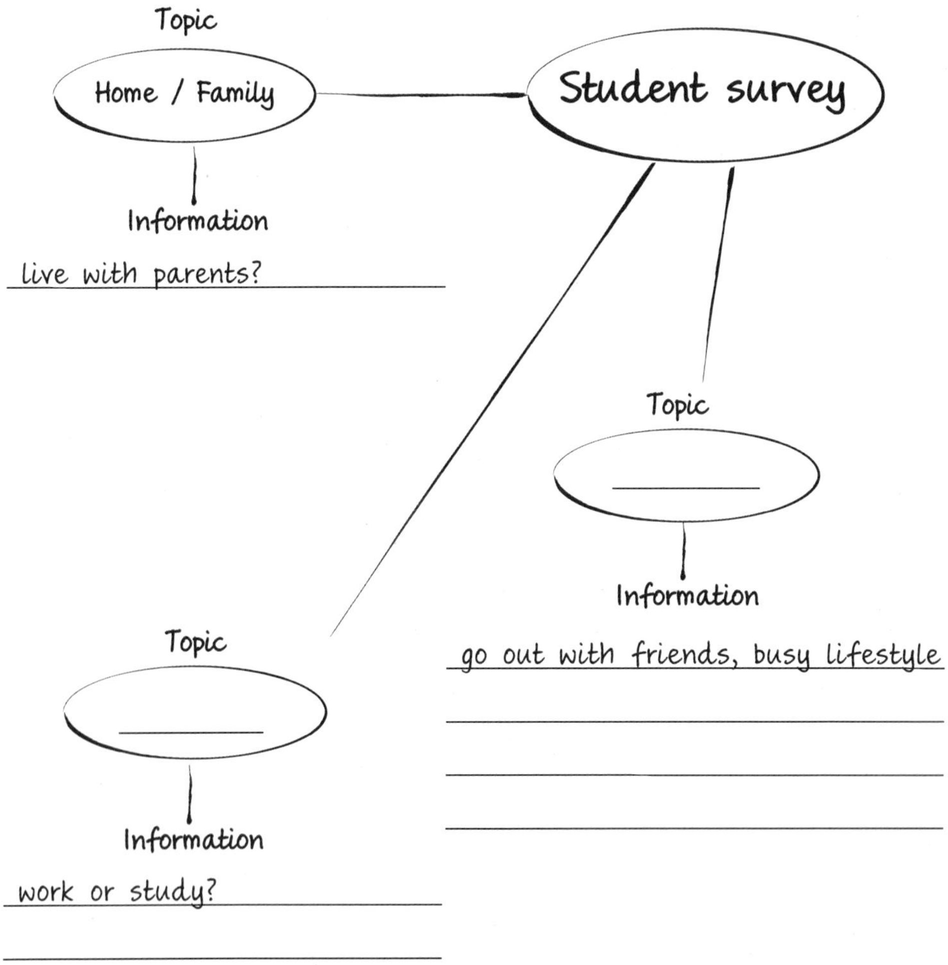
Student survey
Topic
Home / Family
Information
live with parents?
Topic
Information
go out with friends, busy lifestyle
Topic
Information
work or study?

2 Check your ideas map with a partner. Make any necessary changes.

3 Make a survey for a student interview.

Think of topics and information you want to know about for your student survey. Write your topics in the circles of the ideas map. Write the information you want to know about under your topics, e.g. go out with friends, play computer games, etc. Use ideas from Listening 1 and Listening 2 to help you.

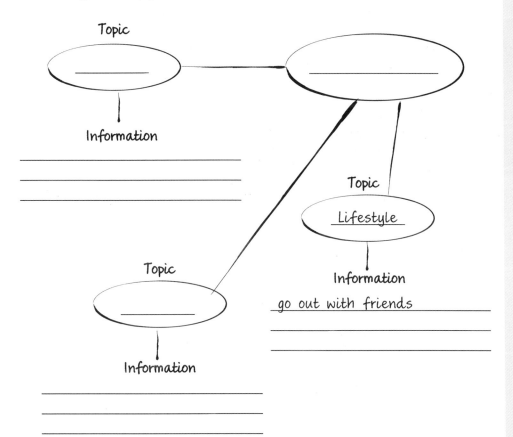

Topic

_____

Information

_____
_____
_____

Topic

_____

Information

_____

Topic

Lifestyle

Information

go out with friends_____
_____
_____

Topic

_____

Information

_____
_____
_____

4 Transform the information from your ideas map into question forms to make questions for your questionnaire.

Yes / no questions: Do you ... ?
Information questions: Where do you _____ ?
                          When do you _____ ?
                          Why do you _____ ?
                          How do you _____ ?
                          Who do you _____ with?

5 Add more questions.

_____
_____
_____

PREPOSITIONS OF TIME

GRAMMAR

Use prepositions to talk about when something happens.

in + parts of the day	**in** the morning, **in** the afternoon, **in** the evening
	I play computer games **in** the evening.
at + clock time	**at** 7:30, **at** 12:00, **at** 1:00 pm
	Luis eats dinner **at** 7:30.
on + day of the week	**on** Monday, **on** Tuesday, **on** Wednesday
	She exercises **on** Monday and Wednesday.

You can use the plural form of the days of the week.
She exercises **on** Mondays and Wednesdays.

1 Read the sentences. Underline …

- *in* + parts of the day.
- *at* + clock time.
- *on* + day of the week.

1 Fahd has breakfast <u>at 6:30 in the morning</u>.
2 Tania gets up at 6:00 in the morning.
3 Chen and Wang watch films in the evening.
4 My sister makes my lunch on Wednesdays.
5 Luis goes home at 3:00 in the afternoon.
6 I play football with my friends on Saturdays.

 PLUS

2 Read this text about a student. Write *in*, *on* or *at* in the gaps.

This is Rabia. She's from Turkey. She takes the bus to the university every day. The bus comes ⁽¹⁾_____ 7:30. Rabia arrives ⁽²⁾_____ 8:30. She has a Biology class ⁽³⁾_____ nine ⁽⁴⁾_____ Tuesday and Thursday. ⁽⁵⁾_____ Wednesday, she has lunch with her friends ⁽⁶⁾_____ 12:30. ⁽⁷⁾_____ Thursday, Rabia has an English class ⁽⁸⁾_____ three o'clock ⁽⁹⁾_____ the afternoon. She goes to the cinema with her family ⁽¹⁰⁾_____ Friday evening. ⁽¹¹⁾_____ Saturday, she exercises ⁽¹²⁾_____ the morning. ⁽¹³⁾_____ Sunday, she does her homework ⁽¹⁴⁾_____ the evening. She has a busy week.

3 🔊 3.6 Listen and check your answers.

PRONUNCIATION FOR SPEAKING

Present simple -s and -es endings

You say /s/ after the sounds /t/, /p/, /k/ and /f/ – *texts, sleeps, takes, laughs.*

You say /z/ after /d/, /l/, /b/, /g/, /v/, /m/, /n/, /r/ and all vowel sounds – *needs, calls, wears, goes, has, studies, plays.*

You say /əz/ after /z/, /t ʃ/, /ʃ/, /s/ and /dʒ/ – *chooses, watches, teaches, misses.*

4 ◀)) 3.7 Listen and repeat.

5 ◀)) 3.7 Listen again. Write the number of syllables next to each word.

texts _____   sleeps _____   needs _____   goes _____
studies _____   watches _____   chooses _____

6 ◀)) 3.8 Listen and tick (✔) the box with the ending you hear.

	/s/	/z/	/əz/
1 gets	✔		
2 wears			
3 misses			
4 has			
5 teaches			
6 takes			
7 plays			
8 laughs			

SPEAKING TASK

Interview students for a survey.

PREPARE

1 Look back at your questions from Exercises 4 and 5 in the Critical thinking section. Review your questions and add any new information you want to include. Share your questions with a partner. Do you like any of your partner's questions? Add them to your survey.

2 Use the polite ways in the box to ask and answer questions in your interview.

Asking	Answering
• Excuse me! Can I ask you some questions?	• Yes, sure. / Yes, no problem.
• I'm ... What's your name?	• Yes. / Yes, I think so.
• I'm ...	• No. / No, not really.
• Nice to meet you!	
• OK, do you ... ?	

3 Read the Task checklist as you prepare your interview.

TASK CHECKLIST	✔
Create questions for a survey.	
Use the present simple to ask and answer questions.	
Use the correct present simple -s and -es endings.	

DISCUSS

4 Work in groups. Interview a student from your group. Take notes to remember your partner's answers to the questions.

5 Work with a partner from another group. Tell your new partner about your first partner's answers. Remember to add -s or -es to your present simple verbs.

OBJECTIVES REVIEW

1 Check your learning objectives for this unit. Write *3, 2* or *1* for each objective.

3 = very well   2 = well   1 = not so well

I can ...

watch and understand a video about a kite festival in Australia.   _____

listen for main ideas.   _____

understand surveys.   _____

use the present simple.   _____

use prepositions to talk about when things happen.   _____

interview students for a survey.   _____

2 Go to the *Unlock* Online Workbook for more practice with this unit's learning objectives.

UNLOCK
ONLINE

WORDLIST		
busy (adj) ⊙	go out (v)	sleep (v) ⊙
café (n)	gym (n)	study (v) ⊙
do homework (v phr)	lifestyle (n) ⊙	teenager (n)
exercise (v) ⊙	parents (n) ⊙	text (v) ⊙
go online (v phr)	play computer games (v phr)	watch TV (v phr)

⊙ = high-frequency words in the Cambridge Academic Corpus

LEARNING OBJECTIVES	IN THIS UNIT YOU WILL ...
Watch and listen	watch and understand a video about Shanghai.
Listening skill	listen for detail.
Critical thinking	interpret maps and directions.
Grammar	use prepositions of place; use the imperative.
Speaking skill	give and ask for directions.
Speaking task	ask for and give directions in a university town.

UNLOCK YOUR KNOWLEDGE

Work with a partner. Ask and answer the questions.

1 What can you see in the photo?
2 Have you been to a place like this?
3 Is it similar to somewhere in your country?

PLUS

WATCH AND LISTEN

PREPARING TO WATCH

ACTIVATING YOUR KNOWLEDGE

1 Work with a partner. Discuss the questions.

1 Do you live in a big city or a small town?
2 How is a city different from a small town?
3 Why do people move to cities?
4 How do cities change?

PREDICTING CONTENT USING VISUALS

2 Look at the pictures from the video. Match the sentences (a–d) to the photos (1–4).

a The man is taking a picture. _____
b Many Asian cities have large populations. _____
c The city is changing. It is growing. _____
d In the past, the city was smaller. _____

GLOSSARY

grow (v) to become larger; to increase in size or amount

record (n) information about or a description of an event, usually on paper or in pictures

skyline (n) the outline of buildings, mountains, etc. against the sky

tower (n) a tall, thin building or structure, for example, the Eiffel Tower in Paris, France and the CN Tower in Toronto, Canada

urban (adj) of or in a city

WHILE WATCHING

3 ▶ Watch the video. Write *T* (true) or *F* (false) next to the statements. Correct the false statements.

_____ 1 More people live in cities today.

_____

_____ 2 Shanghai is one of China's biggest cities.

_____

_____ 3 Mr Yao takes pictures of Shanghai once a year.

_____

_____ 4 The city does not look very different today.

_____

4 ▶ Watch again. Write the missing information.

1 In 1970, only two cities in the world had more than _____ million people.
2 These urban areas are _____ for our future.
3 Mr Yao takes pictures of the Shanghai skyline to make a record of _____ in his hometown.
4 Today the city looks very _____ .

5 Circle the correct answers. Then compare your answers with a partner.

1 There are more jobs in *cities / small towns*.
2 China has *slow-growing / fast-growing* cities.
3 People *do not like / like* to record changes.
4 Cities often change *a little / a lot*.

DISCUSSION

6 Work with a partner. Discuss the questions.

1 What is the tallest building in your city?
2 Has your hometown changed? How has it changed?
3 Why do you think cities change?

LISTENING

PREPARING TO LISTEN

UNDERSTANDING
KEY VOCABULARY

1 You are going to listen to a presentation about a new smartphone app. Before you listen, write the words from the box in the correct gap in the sentences below.

> **building** (n) a house, school, hospital or office
> **directions** (n) information which tells you how to get to a place
> **library** (n) a place where people can come to study and which has a lot of books for people to take home
> **location** (n) where something is
> **map** (n) a picture which shows where countries, towns, roads, rivers, etc. are
> **safe** (adj) not dangerous

1 What is the exact _____ of New York City? Is it in the east or west of the country?
2 I need a quiet place to study and read. I'm going to the _____ after school.
3 This is a dangerous area. It's not _____ to walk here alone at night.
4 I have the _____ to your house. They look easy. I will be there in 20 minutes.
5 I work in a very tall _____ in the city centre.
6 Can you see my country on the _____ ? It's right there. It's very small.

PRONUNCIATION FOR LISTENING

SKILLS

Stress in directions

Stress the words

- *this* and *here* to point to things which are near.
- *that* and *there* to point to things which are not near.

2 🔊 4.1 Listen. Write the words you hear in the correct gap in the sentences.

1 Where is _____ photo from?
2 ... there's a shop _____ and a library _____ .
3 Yes, that's a bank over _____ .
4 The library is _____ .

3 🔊 4.1 Listen again. Are the words you wrote stressed?

4 Work with a partner. Look at the map and discuss the questions.

1 What do you use this map for?
2 Where can you find this map?
3 What places can you see on the map?

USING YOUR
KNOWLEDGE

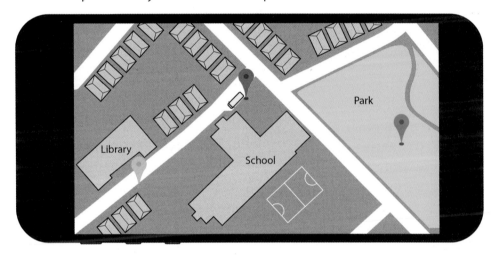

WHILE LISTENING

5 🔊 4.2 Listen to the presentation. Choose the correct answers.

1 Familynet is ...
  a an app for children.
  b an app for work.
  c an app which can find everyone in the family.
2 The presenter says that the map is of ...
  a his home.
  b the locations of his children.
  c his daughters' school.
3 The presentation is about ...
  a how to be safe.
  b how to make parents and children happy.
  c how to find everyone in your family.

LISTENING FOR
MAIN IDEAS

Listening for detail

A *detail* is a fact which gives you information about the main idea.
A detail can be

- a number, a letter or an address.
- a question or an instruction.
- an example of something.

6 🔊 4.2 Listen again. Write *T* (true) or *F* (false) next to the statements.
Correct the false statements.

_____ 1 The salesman says that parents and children are very busy.
_____ 2 The app works all the time.
_____ 3 The app shows locations.
_____ 4 The map shows the locations of two children.
_____ 5 One daughter is between the school and the library.
_____ 6 The teenagers do not like the app.

DISCUSSION

7 Work with a partner. Ask and answer the questions.

1 Would you use Familynet? Why / Why not?
2 Do you think Familynet keeps children safe? Why / Why not?
3 When would Familynet not work?

⊙ LANGUAGE DEVELOPMENT

VOCABULARY FOR PLACES

1 Write the words from the box next to the places (1–10) on Map 1 on page 87.

> **bank** (n) somewhere you can put your money
> **bridge** (n) something which goes over water or a road so people can get from one side to the other
> **factory** (n) a place where workers use machines to make things
> **fountain** (n) a beautiful tower with water coming out of it
> **library** (n) a place with a lot of books
> **monument** (n) something large which people visit to remember an important person or event
> **museum** (n) a place with paintings, statues and important things from history
> **park** (n) a place where you can go for a walk and see a lot of trees and grass
> **train station** (n) somewhere you can get on a train
> **university** (n) a place where students study at a high level after secondary school

Map 1

1 _____

2 _____

3 _____

4 _____

5 _____

6 _____

7 _____

8 _____

9 _____

10 _____

2 🔊 4.3 Listen to eight short conversations. Write the words you hear in the correct gap in the sentences.

1 Where's the _____ ? Is it near here?
2 Is there a _____ near here?
3 Where's the famous _____ ?
4 Excuse me. Where's the _____ ?
5 I can't find the _____ . Is it near here?
6 Where's the _____ ?
7 Where can I find the _____ ?
8 I'm looking for the _____ . Is it in the park?

3 🔊 4.3 Listen again. Match each question from Exercise 2 (1–8) to an answer (a–h).

a Yes, it's behind the river. _____
b Yes. There's one over the bridge. Can you see it? _____
c It's in front of a tall building _____
d It's between the university and the river. _____
e Yes. It's there in the park. _____
f No. It's there on the left. It's next to the park. _____
g It's by the river. _____
h It's opposite those houses. _____

PREPOSITIONS OF PLACE

4 Find these prepositions in Exercise 3 and circle them.

> by   behind   between   in   in front of
> next to   on the left / right   opposite   over

5 Write the prepositions from Exercise 4 under the pictures (1–8). For 1–7, describe the ball's location. There may be more than one answer.

1 _____   2 _____   3 _____   4 _____

5 _____   6 _____   7 _____   8 _____

PLUS

6 Look at Map 2. Write words from the pictures below and Exercise 5 in the gaps.

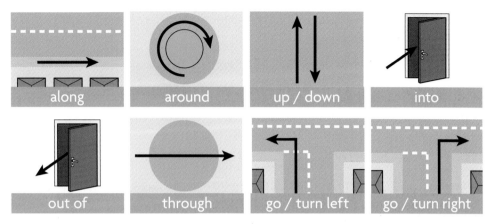

| along | around | up / down | into |
| out of | through | go / turn left | go / turn right |

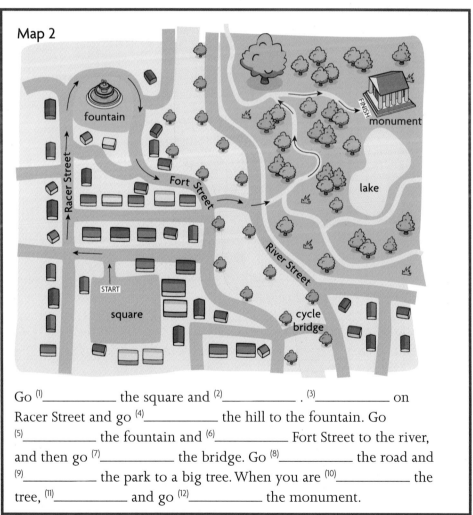

Map 2

Go (1)_____ the square and (2)_____ . (3)_____ on Racer Street and go (4)_____ the hill to the fountain. Go (5)_____ the fountain and (6)_____ Fort Street to the river, and then go (7)_____ the bridge. Go (8)_____ the road and (9)_____ the park to a big tree. When you are (10)_____ the tree, (11)_____ and go (12)_____ the monument.

THE IMPERATIVE

GRAMMAR

Use the imperative to give instructions and directions. There is no pronoun in the imperative. Use the infinitive.

Go along South Road.   **Go** over the bridge. **Turn** right at the bank.

Use *do not / don't* with the imperative to make the negative.

Don't go along South Road. **Don't go** over the bridge.
Don't turn right at the bank.

7 Write the correct imperative from the box in the gaps. You can use some imperatives more than once.

| Go   Turn   Don't forget   Enter   Walk |

1 _____ left on Small Street.
2 _____ down Main Road to get to the bus station.
3 _____ right on Sun Street to get to the park.
4 _____ the building on York Street.
5 _____ to get the directions!
6 _____ left at the library.

8 Correct the mistakes in the sentences.

1 You turn the map the other way, please! I can't read it.

_____

2 Looks for the café on South Road.

_____

3 No enter the building on Main Road.

_____

4 Don't to go along York Street to the gym.

_____

5 Not go east on West Park Street.

_____

6 Don't turns left on Sun Street.

_____

9 Work with a partner. Look at Map 2 on page 89. Use prepositions and the imperative to give different directions from the square to the monument.

PREPARING TO LISTEN

USING YOUR
KNOWLEDGE

1 Work with a partner. Ask and answer the questions.

   a In what places do people get lost (not know where they are)?
   b What can they do to find their way again?

UNDERSTANDING
KEY VOCABULARY

2 Work with a partner. Ask the questions about places in the table.
Add more places below if you can.

- Which of these places did you go to last week?
- Were the places difficult to find?

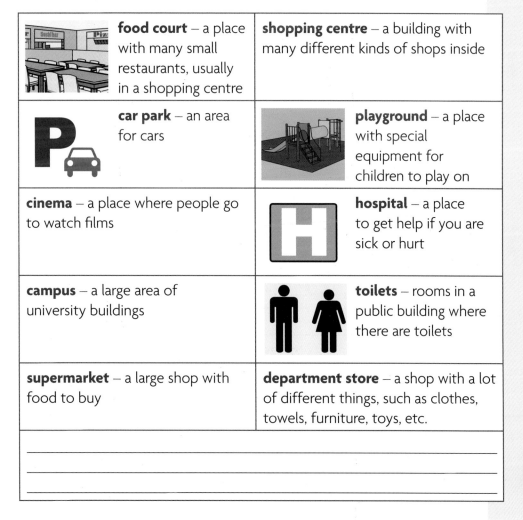

food court – a place with many small restaurants, usually in a shopping centre	**shopping centre** – a building with many different kinds of shops inside
car park – an area for cars	**playground** – a place with special equipment for children to play on
cinema – a place where people go to watch films	**hospital** – a place to get help if you are sick or hurt
campus – a large area of university buildings	**toilets** – rooms in a public building where there are toilets
supermarket – a large shop with food to buy	**department store** – a shop with a lot of different things, such as clothes, towels, furniture, toys, etc.

PLUS

3 You are going to listen to some students answer questions about directions. Before you listen, look at Map 3. What kind of place can you see? Choose the correct answer.

a a map of a shopping centre
b a map of a university campus
c a map of a small town

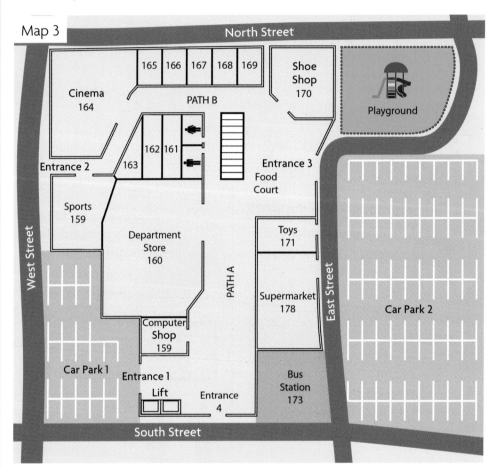

Map 3

North Street

165 | 166 | 167 | 168 | 169

Cinema 164

PATH B

Shoe Shop 170

Playground

162 161

163

Entrance 2

Entrance 3
Food Court

Sports 159

West Street

Department Store 160

Toys 171

PATH A

Supermarket 178

East Street

Car Park 2

Computer Shop 159

Car Park 1

Entrance 1

Lift

Entrance 4

Bus Station 173

South Street

4 Look at Map 3 again. Write *T* (true) or *F* (false) next to the statements. Correct the false statements.

_____ **1** There are two car parks.
_____ **2** There are stairs and a lift in the shopping centre.
_____ **3** The supermarket is between the bus station and South Street.
_____ **4** The playground is behind the shoe shop.
_____ **5** Entrance 3 is on North Street.
_____ **6** The food court is opposite the stairs.
_____ **7** The toilets are in front of the stairs.
_____ **8** There is a bus station on East Street.

WHILE LISTENING

5 🔊 4.4 Listen to some students give directions. Choose the correct answers.

1 The students are …
  a at a shopping centre.
  b lost.
  c looking at a map.

2 The teacher thinks it's important to …
  a know how to find shopping centres.
  b understand map directions.
  c like shopping.

3 Who asks the questions?
  a the teacher
  b the students
  c the teacher and the students

6 🔊 4.4 Listen again. Write the words you hear in the correct gap in the sentences.

1 Teacher: Hassan, I'm at the department store. How do I get to the _____ ?

2 Hassan: Go _____ the shop and go _____ on path A.

3 Teacher: Altan, I'm on North Street. Can you tell me how to get to the _____ ?

4 Altan: Yes, go _____ . Then, turn _____ on East Street and follow it until you see the supermarket. It's on your right, _____ to the bus station.

5 Teacher: Excuse me, miss. Where are the _____ ?

6 Luisa: Oh, that's easy. They're _____ you, _____ to the stairs.

DISCUSSION

7 Work with a partner. Use ideas from Listening 1 and Listening 2. Discuss the questions.

1 In Listening 1, a family uses an app to find each other. In Listening 2, students use a map to find locations in a shopping centre. Would you use the Familynet app in the shopping centre? Why / Why not?

2 What do you do when you get lost on the street? In a shopping centre? In a car park?

3 In Listening 1 and Listening 2, the speakers use words to give directions in the UK. In your culture, when you give directions, do you use …
  • street names and numbers?   • north, south, east and west?
  • km for distance?
  If not, how do you give directions?

4 Do you like to use an app or a map when you travel to a new place? Why / Why not?

SPEAKING

CRITICAL THINKING

At the end of this unit, you are going to do the speaking task below.

Ask for and give directions in a university town.

 UNDERSTAND

1 Circle the words used to describe locations in the sentences.

1 The cinema is (on your right.)
2 I'm in this shoe shop.
3 It's there, on your right, next to the bus station.
4 It's here, behind the food court and the shoe shop.
5 I'm at the cinema.
6 It's opposite you, next to the stairs.

2 Work with a partner. Look at Map 3 of the shopping centre on page 92. Use arrows to draw the quickest way from car park 1 to the playground.

APPLY

3 Use the directions to describe the way from car park 1 to the playground in the correct order.

- When you get to the food court, turn right / turn left.
- Go in Entrance 1 / Entrance 2 / Entrance 3.
- At path A / path B, ...
- Turn left / right.
- It's here / there.
- It's in front of the shoe shop / behind the shoe shop.
- Go along path A / path B.

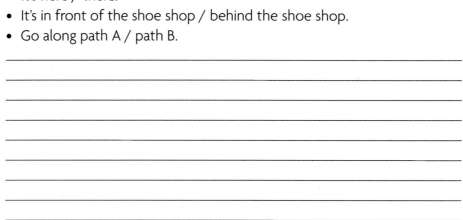

_____
_____
_____
_____
_____
_____
_____
_____
_____

4 Work with a partner. Answer the questions.

    a How do I get from Entrance 2 to the lift?

    b How do I get from the bus station to the shoe shop?

5 Look at Map 3 again. If you are in the bottom left corner of the map (where West Street meets South Street), what is the quickest way to the shoe shop? Check your answers with a partner.

    a Go up West Street, turn right through Entrance 2. Then follow path B.

    b Go through Car Park 1, through Entrance 1. Then follow path A through the food court.

    c Go down South Street, turn left through Entrance 4. Then follow path A through the food court.

 ANALYZE

EVALUATE

PREPARATION FOR SPEAKING

GIVING DIRECTIONS

> **SKILLS**
>
> Give directions by using imperatives and prepositions and describing locations.
>
> Go out of the car park and turn right.
>
> Go north. Then go left on path B. It's next to the department store.

1 Look at the directions from Listening 2. Underline the imperatives used to give directions.

    1 <u>Go</u> out of the shop and <u>go</u> left on path A.

    2 Go east. Then, turn right on East Street and follow it until you see the supermarket.

    3 Go along path B and go through the food court.

2 4.5 Listen and write the words from the box in the correct gap in the sentences.

along	at	behind	in	in front of
next to	on	opposite	right	through

    1 It's _____ the Business school.

    2 It's _____ Green Square.

    3 Go _____ Alpha Park to the Student Centre.

    4 It's _____ that big fountain. There – on the _____ .

    5 OK, then, so we're _____ the Language school.

    6 Go _____ French Road.

    7 There's one _____ the train station.

    8 It's there _____ the left. It's _____ that school.

PLUS

ASKING FOR DIRECTIONS

3 🔊 4.6 Put the words in order to make questions. Then listen and check your answers.

1 the / Where's / supermarket / ?
2 Is the / here / Physics building / near / ?
3 the Language Centre / How / do I / get to / ?
4 how to get / to the History / Can you tell me / building / ?
5 the Maths building / I'm looking for / . / near here / Is it / ?

4 🔊 4.7 Listen to the words in the box and repeat.

> Maths building   Physics building
> Language Centre   Student Centre

5 Work with a partner. Write the words from the box below in the correct gap in the sentences (1–4). Take turns to ask for directions.

> How   Where   to get   near here

1 Excuse me. _____'s the Physics Building?
2 Can you tell me how _____ to the Language Centre?
3 Is there a Student Centre _____?
4 _____ do I get to the Maths Building?

6 🔊 4.8 Listen to three people ask for directions. Write the questions which they ask.

1 Excuse me! _____ , please?
2 Excuse me! I think I'm lost. _____ ?
3 Excuse me! _____ ?

PRONUNCIATION FOR SPEAKING

> ### Pronunciation of phrases
>
> A statement or question has one or more phrases. A phrase has one or two stressed words.
>
> I can't <u>find</u> my <u>car</u>.
> <u>Where's</u> the <u>Physics</u> building?
> <u>How</u> do I get to the <u>food</u> court?

7 🔊 4.9 Listen to these questions. Underline the words or parts of words with stress. (You will hear each phrase by itself, then the whole question.)

1 Excuse me!	Where's the	Student Centre, please?	
2 Excuse me!	I think I'm lost.	How do I get to	the Chemistry building?
3 Excuse me!	Can you tell me	how to get to	the supermarket?

8 🔊 4.9 Listen again. Does the voice go up or down in the phrases and questions? Write (↗ or ↘) in the spaces.

1 Where's the Student Centre, please? _____
2 How do I get to the Chemistry building? _____
3 Can you tell me how to get to the supermarket? _____

9 🔊 4.9 Listen again. Repeat each phrase you hear. Then repeat the whole question.

10 Work in pairs. Read the phrases and questions in Exercise 8 to your partner. Listen to your partner's questions. Did they stress the right words or parts of words?

SPEAKING TASK

> Ask for and give directions in a university town.

PREPARE

1 You are going to help a group of new students at your university. Look back at the Preparation for speaking section for language you want to include.

2 Read the Task checklist as you prepare your directions.

TASK CHECKLIST	✔
Ask for directions.	
Give directions and use the correct order.	
Use the imperative.	
Use words and phrases to describe location (e.g. *behind*, *on*, *in*, etc.).	
Practise your pronunciation of phrases and stress the correct words.	

PRACTISE

3 Work in two groups, A and B.

Group A: Go to page 192.
Group B: Go to page 194.

DISCUSS

4 Work with a student from the other group from Exercise 3 on page 98.

Student A: Look at the map of The University of Beta below. Ask Student B for directions to the places (1–5). Write the correct letter (A–E) next to each place.

Student B: Look at the map on page 194 again. Give directions to Student A.

The University of Beta

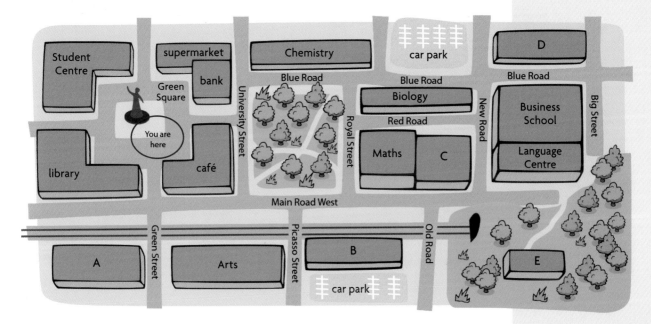

1 the train station _____

2 the gym _____

3 the bus station _____

4 the History building _____

5 the Physics building _____

5 Change roles.

Student B: Look at the map of The University of Alpha. Ask Student A for directions to the places (1–5). Write the correct letter (A–E) next to each place.

Student A: Look at the map on page 192. Give directions to Student B.

The University of Alpha

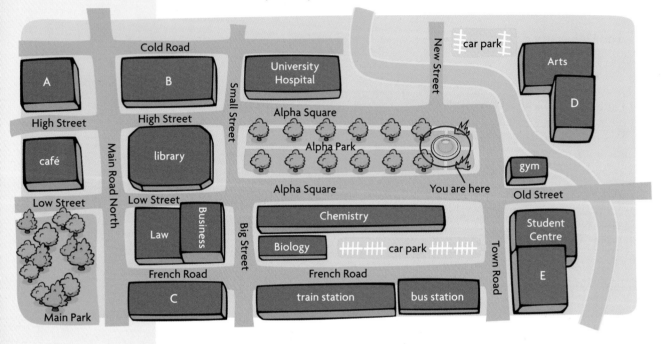

1 the History building _____
2 the Physics building _____
3 the supermarket _____
4 the Language Centre _____
5 the bank _____

6 Use the maps on pages 192 and 194 to check your answers together.

OBJECTIVES REVIEW

1 Check your learning objectives for this unit. Write *3, 2* or *1* for each objective.

   3 = very well   2 = well   1 = not so well

   I can ...

   watch and understand a video about Shanghai.   _____

   listen for detail.   _____

   interpret maps and directions.   _____

   use prepositions of place.   _____

   use the imperative.   _____

   give and ask for directions.   _____

   ask for and give directions in a university town.   _____

2 Go to the *Unlock* Online Workbook for more practice with this unit's learning objectives.

UNLOCK **ONLINE**

WORDLIST		
bank (n) ⊙	fountain (n)	record (n) ⊙
bridge (n) ⊙	grow (v) ⊙	safe (adj) ⊙
building (n) ⊙	hospital (n) ⊙	shopping centre (n)
campus (n)	library (n) ⊙	skyline (n)
car park (n)	location (n) ⊙	supermarket (n)
cinema (n)	map (n) ⊙	toilets (n pl)
department store (n)	monument (n) ⊙	tower (n) ⊙
directions (n pl) ⊙	museum (n) ⊙	train station (n)
factory (n) ⊙	park (n) ⊙	university (n) ⊙
food court (n)	playground (n)	urban (adj) ⊙

⊙ = high-frequency words in the Cambridge Academic Corpus

LEARNING OBJECTIVES	IN THIS UNIT YOU WILL ...
Watch and listen	watch and understand a video about a dangerous job.
Listening skill	use your knowledge to predict content; listen for opinions.
Critical thinking	identify criteria.
Grammar	use *have to*; use *should*; use comparative adjectives.
Speaking skills	compare people; ask for and give opinions and reasons; make a decision.
Speaking task	choose a person for a job.

JOBS

UNL⟲CK YOUR KNOWLEDGE

1 Which job can you see in the photo?

2 Which adjectives describe the job in the photo?

> boring   dangerous   difficult   easy   interesting   safe

PLUS

3 Would you like to do this job? Why / Why not?

ACTIVATING YOUR KNOWLEDGE

PREDICTING CONTENT USING VISUALS

PREPARING TO WATCH

1 Match the buildings (1–4) to the cities (a–d).

1	Empire State Building	a	Dubai
2	Eiffel Tower	b	New York
3	Burj Khalifa	c	Kuala Lumpur
4	Petronas Towers	d	Paris

2 Look at the pictures from the video. Put the words in order to make sentences.

1 very / is / tall / The building / .
2 beautiful view / This building / a / has / .
3 The man / a / very dangerous / job / has / .
4 work / together / These / men / .

GLOSSARY

careful (adj) giving attention to something

dirty (adj) not clean

exciting (adj) making you feel interested; not boring

ground (n) the surface of the Earth

WHILE WATCHING

UNDERSTANDING
MAIN IDEAS

3 ▶ Watch the video. Choose the correct answers.

1 Where is the world's tallest building?
   a Beijing
   b Dubai
   c Mexico City

2 What is a problem with the building?
   a It is taller than any other building.
   b The men cannot clean it.
   c Its windows get dirty.

3 How long does it take to clean all the windows?
   a three months
   b fifteen days
   c one week

UNDERSTANDING
DETAIL

4 ▶ Watch again. Write T (true) or F (false) next to the statements. Correct the false statements.

_____ 1 The Burj Khalifa is over 1,800 metres tall.
_____ 2 The men work thousands of feet above the ground.
_____ 3 The men clean 24,000 doors.
_____ 4 Johnny's team has a dangerous, but exciting job.

MAKING INFERENCES

5 Write the phrases from the box in the correct column of the table.

| have / has many offices   have / has a dangerous job |
| is / are very famous   need / needs special training |

the window washers	the building
1 _____	3 _____
2 _____	4 _____

DISCUSSION

6 Work with a partner. Discuss the questions.

1 Do you, or someone you know, have a dangerous or exciting job? What is it?
2 What are some other dangerous jobs?
3 Why do you think some people like dangerous jobs?

LISTENING

PREPARING TO LISTEN

UNDERSTANDING
KEY VOCABULARY

1 You are going to listen to a student who needs to decide what job to do. Before you listen, write the words from the box in the correct gap in the sentences below. Change the verbs to the correct form.

---

advice (n) suggestions about what you think someone should do
boring (adj) not interesting or exciting
earn (v) to get money for doing work
hard (adj) difficult to do
help (v) to make it easier for someone to do something
job (n) the work a person does to get money
work (v) to do a job, especially a job you do to get money

---

1 I have to _____ more hours this week because I was on holiday last week.
2 Who _____ more money – a doctor or an engineer?
3 She has a very good _____ . It pays well. She makes more money than I do.
4 She's a doctor. She _____ people get better when they are ill.
5 I don't think that job is interesting. It would be _____ to do it every day.
6 You have to study for many years and be good at science to become a doctor. That sounds _____ to me.
7 He has to decide what to do. He should ask his parents for _____ .

Using your knowledge to predict content

Before you listen to a talk or a conversation, answer these questions.

- What is the topic?
- What do you know about the topic?

Thinking about your knowledge of the topic helps you understand what you hear.

USING YOUR KNOWLEDGE

2 Work with a partner. Discuss the questions.

1 What is more important to you in a job? Use the words in the box to help you.

> helping others   kind of job   money   working hours

2 How do people choose their jobs?

3 Who do you talk to when you need to decide something important?

3 Match the jobs (1–6) to the correct pictures (a–f).

1 businesswoman _____   4 doctor _____

2 chef _____   5 musician _____

3 engineer _____   6 scientist _____

4 Answer the questions about the jobs in Exercise 3. Use your own ideas.

Who ...

1 works harder than other people? *a chef*
2 helps people?
3 has a more interesting job?
4 earns more money?

PRONUNCIATION FOR LISTENING

Weak form *have to*

Words in a sentence are pronounced either with stress or no stress. The main verb, the subject and the object are usually stressed (strong form). Words such as auxiliary verbs, prepositions and articles are usually unstressed (weak form).

When *have* is the main verb, we use the strong form and the final sound is *v*. When we use *have to* before another verb, we use the weak form. The letter *v* sounds like *f*. The preposition *to* is not usually stressed.

I have two computers.   I have **to** work on Mondays.
  (v)   (f) (tə)

When *has* is the main verb, it is stressed and the final sound is *z*. When we use *has to* before another verb, the letter *s* in *has* sounds like *z*. The preposition *to* is not usually stressed.

He has two jobs.   He has **to** get up at 5:30.
  (z)   (s) (tə)

🔊 5.1 Look at the four sentences above again. Listen to how they are pronounced.

5 🔊 5.2 Listen and decide if *have/has* are in the weak or strong form.

1 I *have to* choose a course. *weak / strong*
2 I *have two* questions to ask you. *weak / strong*
3 You *have to* work hard. *weak / strong*
4 He *has to* study at university. *weak / strong*
5 He *has two* options: Maths or Biology. *weak / strong*
6 She *has to* decide what to do. *weak / strong*
7 You *have to* do four subjects. *weak / strong*

WHILE LISTENING

> **GLOSSARY**
>
> **grade** (n) a number or letter that shows how good someone's work is
>
> **careers adviser** (n) someone who gives advice about jobs to secondary school students
>
> **medical school** (n) a school where students study to become doctors

6 🔊 5.3 Listen and choose the correct answers.

1 Who is the student with?
   a her friend
   b her careers adviser
   c her mother

2 When is the student going to university?
   a next year
   b this year
   c next month

3 What does the student ask for?
   a money
   b to be a musician
   c advice about what to study

4 The adviser says Beatrice has _____ .
   a good grades
   b nice parents
   c a good job

SKILLS

Listening for opinions

An opinion is an idea about a person, place, thing or event. We can use *should* to give advice and *think* to give an opinion.

What **should** I **do**? **Should** I **get** a job?
You **should work** hard.
I **think** you **should go** to college.
I **don't think** you **should become** a chef.

7 🔊 5.3 Listen again. What should Beatrice do next year? What is each person's opinion? Take notes.

Mother: _____
_____
_____

Father: _____
_____
_____

Adviser: _____
_____
_____

DISCUSSION

8 Work with a partner. Ask and answer the questions.

1 Would you like to do any of the jobs in Exercise 3? Why / Why not?
2 What skills do you need for these jobs?

PLUS

HAVE TO / HAS TO

GRAMMAR

Use *have to / has to* + the infinitive to show that something is necessary.

I / you / we / they	have to	be	helpful.
He / she / it	has to	get up	early.

Nurses **have to be** helpful.
A teacher **has to get up** early.

Use *don't / doesn't have to* + the infinitive to show that something is not necessary.

I / you / we / they	do not / don't	have to	be	helpful.
He / she / it	does not / doesn't	have to	get up	early.

Nurses **don't have to be** women.
A doctor **doesn't have to work** in a hospital.

Use *do / does* + subject + *have to* + the infinitive to ask if something is necessary.
Do we **have to leave** now?   **Does** she **have to be** a doctor?

Be careful! *Have* and *have to* don't have the same meaning.
Notice the difference:
I **have to** get a job. I need money.   I **have** a job. I work from 9 to 5.

1 🔊 5.4 Write the words from the box in the correct gap in the sentences. Listen and check.

has   has to   have   have to

1 Fatima _____ two jobs.
2 Mark _____ work very hard.
3 I _____ a very good job.
4 Engineers _____ a difficult job.
5 Paul _____ an important job.
6 Builders _____ work fast.

2 Correct the mistakes in the sentences.

1 Students have read a lot of books.

_____

2 My teacher have to walk to school.

_____

3 You don't have study English.

_____

4 Teachers don't to work at night.

_____

5 Have we learn this grammar?

_____

6 What does a nurse has to do?

_____

3 Work with a partner. Choose one of these jobs. What do people with this job have to do?

| chef   journalist   scientist   football player |

4 Work with a new partner. Repeat Exercise 3, choosing a different job.

SHOULD

PLUS

GRAMMAR

Use *should* + the infinitive to make suggestions or give advice.
I / you / he / she / we / they **should** go to medical school.
Use *should not/shouldn't* + the infinitive in the negative.
I / you / he / she / we / they **should not** / **shouldn't** go to medical school.

5 Correct the mistakes in the sentences.

1 Paul should goes to Medical school.

_____

2 Beatrice not should get a job next year.

_____

3 Laura shoulds ask for advice from her friend.

_____

4 The students no shouldn't miss their classes.

_____

COMPARATIVE ADJECTIVES

Use comparative adjectives + *than* to compare two or more things.

Add *-er* to one-syllable adjectives.	Medicine is **harder than** Engineering. (hard → hard**er**)
For one-syllable adjectives that end in *-e*, add *-r*.	This job is **safer than** that job. (safe → safe**r**)
For two-syllable adjectives that end in *-y*, replace *-y* with *-ier*.	This class is **easier than** my other class. (easy → eas**ier**)
For short adjectives that end in a consonant, double the final consonant and add *-er*.	I am **bigger than** my yoga teacher. (big → bi**gger**)
For adjectives with two or more syllables, do not add *-er*. Put *more* before the adjective.	Computer science is **more interesting than** Medicine. (interesting → **more interesting**)
Some comparative adjectives are irregular: good → better bad → worse	I think this job is **better than** that job. (good → **better**) This job is **worse than** the one I had before. (bad → **worse**)

6 ◀))) 5.5 Listen and repeat the adjectives. Write the number of syllables you hear. Listen again and check your answers.

1 boring _____
2 interesting _____
3 safe _____
4 easy _____
5 difficult _____

6 nice _____
7 big _____
8 small _____
9 good _____
10 important _____

7 Write the comparative form of the adjectives from Exercise 6.

1 _____
2 _____
3 _____
4 _____
5 _____

6 _____
7 _____
8 _____
9 _____
10 _____

8 Complete each sentence with the comparative form of the adjective in brackets + *than* in the gaps.

1 My boss's office is _____ mine. (big)

2 Being a football player is _____ being an engineer. (easy)

3 Walking to work in the morning is _____ walking home at night. (safe)

4 Jen's new job is _____ her old one. (interesting)

5 Working alone is _____ working in a group. (boring)

6 Eduardo's grades this year are _____ they were last year. (good)

📱 PLUS

9 Write comparative adjectives from Exercise 6 in the sentences. Give your opinions.

1 I think studying Medicine is _____ than Business.

2 A nurse's job is usually _____ than a chef's.

3 Working in an office is _____ than working in a shop.

4 A scientist's job is _____ than a musician's.

5 Working in the morning is _____ than working at night.

6 Being a student is _____ than having a job.

LISTENING 2

PREPARING TO LISTEN

USING YOUR
KNOWLEDGE

1 What is most important when you choose a new person for a job?

   a what the person is like
   b what the person knows

UNDERSTANDING
KEY VOCABULARY

2 Read the sentences and choose the best definition for the words in bold.

   1 Robert is very **strong**. He can lift heavy things, so he is a good builder.
      a not physically powerful
      b physically powerful
   2 Alissa is a very **kind** doctor. She cares a lot about her patients and wants them to feel good.
      a wanting to help others and show you care about them
      b very unpleasant and not friendly
   3 Tomas is **polite**. He always says 'please' and 'thank you' to people.
      a behaving in a way which shows good manners and respect for others
      b showing bad manners and no respect for others
   4 An engineer's job is a good **example** of a job which makes a lot of money.
      a something which is the opposite of what you are talking about
      b something which is typical of what you are talking about
   5 Juan is **fit** because he goes to the gym every day and eats healthy food.
      a healthy and strong, especially from exercising
      b not healthy and doesn't exercise
   6 Alex wants to **teach** people how to cook.
      a to learn about new things
      b to give lessons at a school or university

 PLUS

3 You are going to listen to two managers choose someone for a job. Before you listen, read the job posting and answer the questions.

1 Where is the job?
2 What is the job?
3 What kind of person should apply?

UNIVERSITY OF YUKON

Home

Jobs

Register for job ads

Manage job alerts

FAQ

Contact us

Home > Jobs > Current vacancies

About us

The UoY sports centre is for students and staff at UoY. We have a gym, a swimming pool, tennis courts, a football pitch and a basketball court.

We have courses in yoga, pilates, zumba, kung-fu, running, cycling, swimming and much more.

**Fitness instructor
(Ref: UoY-SSv/SpC-0098)**

The UoY sports centre is looking for a new fitness instructor. We are looking for a person who:

- can teach sports and exercise.
- is friendly and helpful.
- has experience.

About you

You should:

- be strong and fit.
- know three or more sports.
- speak English and French.

Click **here** to apply.

4 Work with a partner. Read about a person who wants the job. Then ask and answer the questions below.

Student A: Go to page 193.

Student B: Go to page 195.

1 Is it a man or a woman?
2 What's his / her name?
3 Where's he / she from?
4 What languages does he / she speak?
5 What sports can he / she teach?

5 Tell your partner about your person. Who should get the job?

WHILE LISTENING

LISTENING FOR MAIN IDEAS

GLOSSARY

experience (n) knowledge which you get from doing a job

6 🔊 5.6 Listen to two managers choose a new fitness instructor. Who do they choose, Alan or Lucy?

Alan   Lucy

7 ◀)) 5.6 Read the questions. Then listen again and choose the correct answers.

1 What other job do they talk about?
   a nurse
   b scientist
   c doctor
2 Paul thinks a good fitness instructor should …
   a be a good student.
   b be a good teacher.
   c teach tennis.
3 Paul likes Lucy because she's …
   a a good scientist.
   b Canadian.
   c a fitness instructor.
4 Emma thinks a fitness instructor has to be …
   a friendly and helpful.
   b strong and fit.
   c kind and polite.
5 Emma thinks Alan can help students …
   a work hard.
   b be polite.
   c have good ideas.
6 Paul thinks Lucy is better because she …
   a has experience.
   b can teach popular sports.
   c can speak Cantonese.

DISCUSSION

8 Ask and answer the questions with a partner.

1 Do you agree with Paul? Why / Why not?
2 What can happen in the workplace if managers choose the wrong person for a job?
3 Compare the jobs people talk about in Listening 1 and Listening 2. What experience do you need to have for the jobs? How is the experience for the jobs similar or different?
4 In both Listening 1 and Listening 2, people hear advice from others. Do the people follow the advice? Do you think they make the right decisions? Why / Why not?

SPEAKING

CRITICAL THINKING

At the end of this unit, you are going to do the speaking task below.

> Choose a person for a job.

SKILLS

Identifying criteria

Criteria are reasons for doing something. Before you make a decision, think about your criteria. Here are two examples of criteria from Listening 2:

I want a person who has experience – a person who can teach me tennis or volleyball.

We want a person who can make the students work hard.

1 Read about a job and answer the questions.

APPLY

  1 What is the job?

  2 What are the job criteria?

  3 What kind of person does the sports centre want?

  4 Would you be a good person for the job? Why / Why not?

UNIVERSITY OF YUKON

Home

Jobs

Register for job ads

Manage job alerts

FAQ

Contact us

Home > Jobs > **Current vacancies**

Sports Centre Nurse (Ref: UoY-SSv/SpC-0099)

The UoY sports centre is looking for a new nurse. The nurse works closely with other staff and helps our students stay healthy. We are looking for a person who:

- has experience in a hospital.
- speaks another language.
- knows about sport.
- is a hard worker.

About you

You should:

- be helpful.
- like sport.
- be friendly.

The job is full time and includes some nights and weekends.

Click **here** to apply.

2 Work in a group of three. On page 121 read about a person who is applying for the nurse's job at the University of Yukon sports centre. In the table, take notes about your person. Then share the information with your group.

Student A: Read about Inesh.
Student B: Read about Morena.
Student C: Read about Darren.

In the first column, write the job criteria from Exercise 1 on page 119. How well does each person meet the criteria? Give points (0, 1 or 2) and evidence (Note: sometimes there isn't any evidence).

0 = no experience   1 = some experience   2 = good experience

criteria	Inesh	Morena	Darren
has experience in a hospital	Points: Evidence:	Points: Evidence:	Points: 2 Evidence: nurse in a big hospital
	Points: Evidence:	Points: Evidence:	Points: Evidence:
	Points: Evidence:	Points: Evidence:	Points: Evidence:
	Points: Evidence:	Points: Evidence:	Points: Evidence:
helpful and friendly	Points: Evidence:	Points: Evidence:	Points: Evidence:

Student A

Home > Jobs > Current vacancies

About you

My name's Inesh and I'm from Jakarta, Indonesia. I speak four languages: Indonesian, Chinese, Spanish and English. I speak Spanish better than English.

I'm studying to be a nurse in a big hospital in Jakarta.

I'm polite and friendly. This is important because nurses have to help doctors and work with patients.

I would like to go to Canada and work in your sports centre after I get my degree.

UNIVERSITY OF YUKON

Student B

Home > Jobs > Current vacancies

About you

My name's Morena and I'm from São Paulo in Brazil. I speak Portuguese, Spanish and English.

I'm a nurse in a children's hospital. I like working with children, but I would like to work in your sports centre in Canada.

I'm a friendly and helpful nurse. I love sport. I go running and do yoga. I'm strong and fit. This is important because nurses have to work hard.

UNIVERSITY OF YUKON

Student C

Home > Jobs > Current vacancies

About you

My name's Darren and I'm from Chicago, Illinois, in the USA. I'm a nurse in a big hospital. I work hard and I'm good at my job.

I don't speak French, but I'm a fast learner and a good student.

I'm fit and healthy. I love football and basketball, and I go to a gym. This is important because a sports centre nurse should play sports.

I would like to live in Canada.

UNIVERSITY OF YUKON

PREPARATION FOR SPEAKING

PRONUNCIATION FOR SPEAKING

WEAK SOUNDS IN COMPARATIVES

1 🔊 5.7 Listen and repeat the comparative adjectives with the weak form /ə/.

> stronger   faster   harder   safer   kinder

CONSONANTS IN *HAVE TO, HAS TO, HAVE* AND *HAS*

2 🔊 5.8 Listen to the sentences. How do we pronounce the letters in bold below? Match the verbs (1–4) to the correct sound (a–d).

_____ 1 have to   a /f/
_____ 2 has to   b /v/
_____ 3 have   c /z/
_____ 4 has   d /s/

COMPARING

3 Write the words from the box in the correct gap in the sentences with information about Inesh, Morena and Darren. Sometimes you need two words.

> better   bigger   experience   languages   more (× 2)

1 Inesh speaks _____ _____ than Darren.
2 Morena and Darren have _____ _____ as nurses than Inesh.
3 Morena and Darren are _____ at sports than Inesh.
4 Darren works in a _____ hospital than Morena.

ASKING FOR AND GIVING OPINIONS AND REASONS

4 Look at the ways to ask for opinions and give opinions and reasons.
Write the correct phrases in the gaps in the dialogue below. Use the
phrases in the table to help you.

asking for opinions	giving opinions	giving reasons
What do you think about ... ?	I think that ... should be ...	Because he / she ...
Why do you think that?	I think that ...	Another reason is ...

A: What _____ think about Lucy?

B: I think that she _____ be the new fitness instructor.

A: Why _____ think that?

B: _____ she is a better teacher than Alan. Another
_____ is the fitness instructor has to teach
popular sports.

5 Write a conversation similar to the one in Exercise 4. Ask for an opinion
about Inesh.

A: _____
(Ask for an opinion.)

B: _____
(Give an opinion.)

A: _____
(Ask for a reason for an opinion.)

B: _____
(Give two reasons for the opinion.)

MAKING A DECISION

> When you are trying to make a group decision, you can use this language:
> *We need to make a decision.*
> *Let's review our ideas.*
> *So, do we all agree ... ?*
> *Is everyone OK with this decision?*
> *I'm not sure. Can we discuss this a little more?*

6 Look at the discussion. Underline the language for making decisions.

A: OK, everyone, we need to make a decision about where to take
Lucy for dinner. We really want her to take the job, so let's choose
a great place!

B: That's true! So, let's review our ideas.

C: Right. Well, the Japanese restaurant has great food, but it's
very expensive.

A: True. The seafood place is wonderful, but not everyone likes fish.

B: *Joe's Grill* has lots of different kinds of food, it's fun and it's not too expensive. But it's kind of noisy.

A: Well, I recommend that we go to the Japanese restaurant. Yes, it's expensive, but this is an important dinner. Is everyone OK with this decision?

7 Work in a small group. Imagine you are going to choose a new teacher for your class. The teacher can be any famous person in the world. Discuss ideas with your classmates, and then make a decision. Use expressions for making decisions.

SPEAKING TASK

▶ Choose a person for a job.

PREPARE

1 Review your notes in Exercise 2 in the Critical thinking section about how well each person meets the job criteria.

2 Read the Task checklist as you prepare your discussion.

TASK CHECKLIST	✔
Use notes comparing your person to the nurse's job criteria.	
Ask for opinions, give opinions and give reasons for your opinion.	
Use *should*, *have to* and comparative adjectives.	·
Use /ə/ to pronounce *have to*.	
Use expressions for making a decision.	
Choose the new nurse.	

DISCUSS

3 Work in a small group. Take turns asking for opinions, giving opinions and giving reasons about who should be the new nurse.

4 With your group, decide who should be the new nurse. Tell the class your decision. Give your opinions and reasons.

OBJECTIVES REVIEW

1 Check your learning objectives for this unit. Write *3, 2* or *1* for each objective.

3 = very well   2 = well   1 = not so well

I can ...

watch and understand a video about a dangerous job.   _____

use my knowledge to predict content.   _____

listen for opinions.   _____

identify criteria.   _____

use *have to*.   _____

use *should*.   _____

use comparative adjectives.   _____

compare people.   _____

ask for and give opinions and reasons.   _____

make a decision.   _____

choose a person for a job.   _____

2 Go to the *Unlock* Online Workbook for more practice with this unit's learning objectives.

UNLOCK ONLINE

WORDLIST		
advice (n) Ⓞ	hard (adj) Ⓞ	strong (adj) Ⓞ
boring (adj)	help (v) Ⓞ	teach (v) Ⓞ
earn (v)	job (n) Ⓞ	work (v) Ⓞ
example (n) Ⓞ	kind (adj) Ⓞ	
fit (adj) Ⓞ	polite (adj)	

Ⓞ = high-frequency words in the Cambridge Academic Corpus

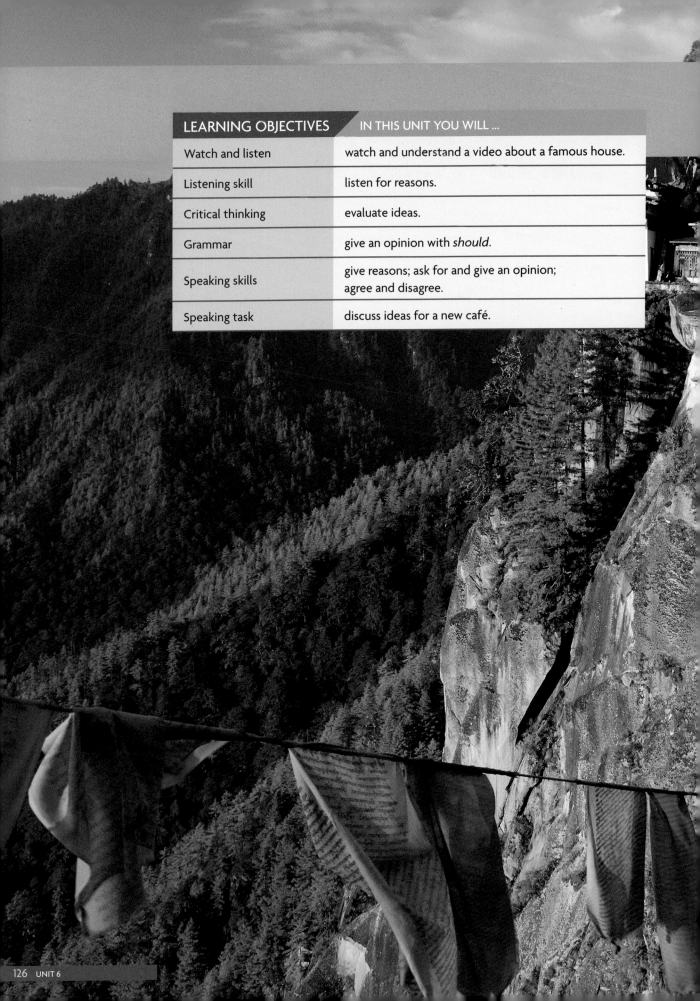

LEARNING OBJECTIVES	IN THIS UNIT YOU WILL ...
Watch and listen	watch and understand a video about a famous house.
Listening skill	listen for reasons.
Critical thinking	evaluate ideas.
Grammar	give an opinion with *should*.
Speaking skills	give reasons; ask for and give an opinion; agree and disagree.
Speaking task	discuss ideas for a new café.

HOMES AND BUILDINGS

UNL⊙CK YOUR KNOWLEDGE

1 Choose three words from the box to describe the photo.

> African   Asian   European   faraway
> interesting   normal   traditional   unusual

2 Would you like to live here? Why / Why not?

3 Would you like to visit this place? Why / Why not?

4 What is special about this place?

PREPARING TO WATCH

ACTIVATING YOUR KNOWLEDGE

1 Work with a partner. Discuss the questions.

1 Do you prefer a small house or a large house? Why?
2 Do you prefer living in a big city or the country? Why?
3 Do you know the names of any famous houses?
4 Where do presidents of countries usually live?
5 Can you name any presidents of the United States?

PREDICTING CONTENT USING VISUALS

2 Look at the pictures from the video. Circle the correct answers.

1 The house is *large / long*.
2 The man is probably *important / modern*.
3 This room is probably a good place to *sleep / study*.
4 There is a *big / small* garden.

GLOSSARY

acre (n) a unit for measuring an outdoor area (1 acre = 0.4 hectare or 10,000 square metres)

convenient (adj) easy to use or suiting your plans well

Declaration of Independence (n) a very important piece of paper in US history, signed on 4 July, 1776

Native American (n) a member of the original groups of people who lived in North and South America

study (n) a room for reading and writing in a person's home

style (n) a way of doing something, especially one that is typical of a person, group of people, place or time.

WHILE WATCHING

3 ▶ Watch the video. Write *T* (true) or *F* (false) next to the statements. Correct the false statements.

UNDERSTANDING MAIN IDEAS

_____ 1 Monticello was the home of Thomas Jefferson.

_____

_____ 2 Jefferson was important to European history.

_____

_____ 3 Monticello has many rooms.

_____

_____ 4 The grounds around the house are not very large.

_____

4 ▶ Watch again. Write the correct words in the gaps.

UNDERSTANDING DETAIL

1 It took more than _____ years to build Monticello.
2 There are items from the New World (the USA) on the _____ in the Indian Hall.
3 A comfortable and _____ house was important for Jefferson.
4 Jefferson usually worked in his _____ in the morning.

5 Match the sentence halves.

MAKING INFERENCES

1 Monticello is   a to hunt.
2 Jefferson did   b were important to Jefferson.
3 Jefferson probably liked   c popular with American tourists.
4 Gardens and green spaces   d a lot of work at home.

DISCUSSION

6 Work with a partner. Discuss the questions.

1 Would you like to live in Monticello? Why / Why not?
2 What's the most famous house in your city or country? Describe it.
3 Describe your dream home.

LISTENING

LISTENING 1

PREPARING TO LISTEN

1 You are going to listen to an interview about designing buildings. Before you listen, work with a partner. Ask and answer the questions.

1 What is your favourite restaurant? What do you like about it?
2 Is the way a restaurant looks as important as the food? Why / Why not?

2 Write the words from the box in the correct gap in the sentences below.

> **ceiling** (n) the top of a room which you can see when you look up
> **floor** (n) what you walk on inside a building
> **furniture** (n) things such as chairs, tables and beds which you put in a home or office
> **room** (n) what the inside of a building is made up of
> **wall** (n) one of the sides of a room
> **wood** (n) the hard material which trees are made of

1 The painting on the _____ is fantastic. It looks like a photo!
2 The old, stone _____ is cold when you walk on it.
3 Look up at the _____ . It's painted to look like the sky!
4 Let's make the tables and chairs out of _____ . I like the colour and it smells like the forest.
5 We will need to buy more _____ so we have enough tables and chairs in the dining room.
6 We need a bigger _____ so we have space for all the new people and things for our business.

PRONUNCIATION FOR LISTENING

Linking words

In English, you connect the end sound of a word with the beginning sound of the next word. This is called 'linking words'. Look at how the consonant sounds are linked to vowel sounds.

Sandy Singh lives_in_India.
Because_it's_a good_idea.

3 ◄)) 6.1 Read the phrases (1–6) from the interview. How do we pronounce the red and blue letters? Listen. Then choose the correct answer (a–c).

1 an author of many books
2 I help architects.
3 For example
4 good ideas
5 restaurants in London
6 What about the UK?

a We do not pronounce the red letters.
b We do not pronounce the blue letters.
c We pronounce the red and blue letters together.

WHILE LISTENING

GLOSSARY

architect (n) someone who designs buildings

design (n) the way something is planned and made

manager (n) someone who is responsible for an office, shop, people, etc.

psychologist (n) someone who knows about people's thoughts and feelings

4 ◄)) 6.2 Listen to an interview on the radio. Choose the correct answers.

1 Dr Thompson is ...
   a a psychologist.
   b an architect.
   c a restaurant manager.
2 Many Mexican restaurants have ...
   a orange walls.
   b red walls.
   c white walls.

3 Many Chinese restaurants have ...
   a orange walls and floors.
   b red walls and floors.
   c white walls and floors.
4 The main topic of the interview is ...
   a older buildings.
   b colours and feelings.
   c good food in restaurants.

LISTENING FOR
MAIN IDEAS

Listening for reasons

Reasons are facts or opinions about why something happens. Speakers often use the words *why* and *because* to give reasons. If we don't give reasons, people may not believe what we say. Listen carefully when you hear the words *why* and *because*.

LISTENING
FOR DETAIL

5 Match the questions (1–5) to the correct reasons (a–e).

questions

1 Why is colour important?
2 Why do many restaurants in Mexico have orange walls?
3 Why don't many restaurants in London have orange walls?
4 Why do many Chinese restaurants have red walls?
5 Why is white a good colour for a British restaurant?

reasons

a Because this is the colour of fire and good things.
b Because it changes the way people think and feel.
c Because colours mean different things in different countries.
d Because this colour makes people feel hungry.
e Because this colour means fresh and clean.

6 🔊 6.2 Listen again and check your answers.

DISCUSSION

7 Work with a partner. Ask and answer the questions.

1 What is your favourite colour? Why?
2 Are there any colours you don't like? Why?
3 Imagine you have a restaurant. What colour do you want the walls to be? Why?

VOCABULARY FOR FURNITURE

1 🔊 6.3 Listen to the words for the furniture in the photos. Repeat.

armchair

table

chair

bookcase

lamp

desk

sofa

PLUS

2 Work with a partner. Take turns asking and answering the questions about the furniture in the photos in Exercise 1. Write your answers in the table.

Are there usually (desks) in a café?
Are there usually (desks) in a home?
Are there (desks) in our classroom?

café	home	our classroom
	desk	

ADJECTIVES FOR FURNITURE

3 Look at the words in the box. They are adjectives which can describe furniture. Some words are both adjectives and nouns.

> **comfortable** (adj) comfortable furniture and clothes make you feel relaxed
>
> **glass** (adj, n) a hard, see-through material used to make windows, bottles, etc.
>
> **leather** (adj, n) the skin of animals used to make things such as shoes and bags
>
> **metal** (adj, n) a hard, shiny material used to make knives and forks, bicycles, machines, etc.
>
> **plastic** (adj, n) a material which can be made into different shapes, e.g. water bottles
>
> **uncomfortable** (adj) not feeling comfortable and pleasant
>
> **wooden** (adj) made of wood

4 🔊 6.4 Listen and repeat the words.

5 Match the pictures to the words in Exercise 3.

_____plastic_____ _____ _____

_____ _____ _____

_____

6 Work with a partner. Take turns to ask and answer the question to describe the furniture in Exercise 1 on page 133.

What's this?   It's a ... comfortable armchair. / I'm not sure.

7 Write the adjectives you used to describe the furniture in Exercise 6.

a _comfortable_ armchair   a _____ lamp

a _____ table   a _____ desk

a _____ chair   a _____ sofa

a _____ bookcase

📱 PLUS

PREPARING TO LISTEN

UNDERSTANDING KEY VOCABULARY

1 You are going to listen to two men discussing ideas for a new building. Before you listen, write the words from the box in the correct gap in the sentences below.

> **cheap** (adj) not costing a lot of money
> **expensive** (adj) costing a lot of money
> **far** (adv) not close to somewhere
> **modern** (adj) using the newest ideas, design, technology, etc.
> **near** (adv, prep) very close to somewhere
> **noisy** (adj) making a lot of noise
> **quiet** (adj) making little noise or no noise

1 This hotel costs a lot of money. It's very _____ .
2 The restaurant is very _____ – people are talking and music is playing.
3 The library is _____ . There isn't much noise there, so we can study a bit better.
4 I like the new building! It's very _____ and looks really different and new.
5 You only have to walk a short way to the train station. It's _____ your building.
6 That place wouldn't be good because you have to drive 30 minutes or more to get there. It's very _____ from everything.
7 This hotel doesn't cost a lot of money. It's very _____ .

USING YOUR KNOWLEDGE

2 Work with a partner. Discuss the questions and give reasons for your answers. Do you and your partner agree or disagree?

1 Do you prefer modern or old buildings? Modern or old furniture?
2 Would you prefer a house in the city or in the country?

WHILE LISTENING

3 🔊 6.5 Look at the map of a town. Then listen to two men discussing ideas for a new building and choose the correct answers.

LISTENING FOR
MAIN IDEAS

1 What kind of building do they discuss?
   a a train station
   b a new office
   c a new hotel

2 Where is the new building going to be?
   a near the train station
   b in the city centre
   c near the park

3 Which of these statements is true?
   a They agree on every idea.
   b They agree on some ideas.
   c They don't agree on any ideas.

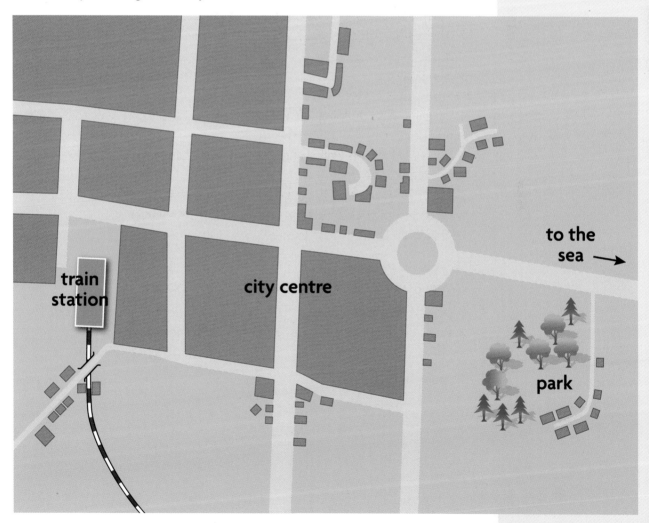

4 🔊 6.5 Listen again. Circle the correct word.

1 The windows are going to be *big / small*.
2 The walls are going to be *blue / yellow*.
3 The desks are going to be made of metal and *wood / plastic*.
4 The chairs are going to be *plastic / comfortable*.

5 Work in groups. Compare your answers. Are they the same?

DISCUSSION

6 Work with a partner. Discuss the questions.

1 Do you agree with the two men? Why / Why not?
2 Think of rooms where you study and work. What is the design? What is
   the colour? How do you feel there? What would you like to change
   about the design?
3 Think about Listening 1 and Listening 2. Would you like to work with
   a psychologist to design a room or building? Why / Why not?
4 Imagine you are going to get an office. What is most important to you:
   the location, the design or the colour inside? Rank them in order (1–3).

SPEAKING

CRITICAL THINKING

At the end of this unit, you are going to do the speaking task below.

> Discuss ideas for a new café.

1 Look at the photos of three cafés. Which café ...

ANALYZE

    1 has an expensive design with a lot of wood? _____
    2 is noisy and in the centre of a city? _____
    3 is beautiful and quiet? _____

Café A

Café B

Café C

SKILLS

Evaluating ideas

When you try to decide your opinion about a topic, think about reasons for it (positive) and against it (negative). This is called *evaluating*. It is helpful to write your ideas in a list or table.

2 Look at the cafés in Exercise 1. In the table, write positive and negative things about each café.

	positive things	negative things
Café A		
Café B		
Café C		

3 Look at the map of Green Town and read the information below it.

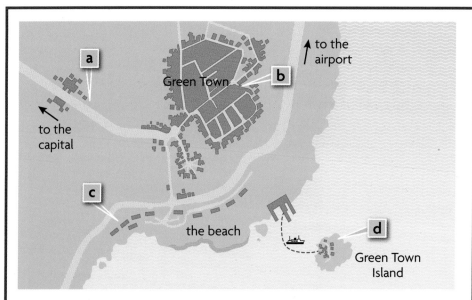

You are going to open a new café in Green Town. Green Town is a small town near the sea. There are two busy roads near the town. One road goes to the capital and the other goes to the airport. Green Town is very popular with tourists. Tourists come from the capital and from countries around the world. There are ten big hotels on the beach. Green Town Island is also popular. Many tourists go on a day trip to the island. Other tourists stay in one of the island's three small hotels. Here are four places for your café:

a near the busy main road
b in the town
c on the beach
d on Green Town Island

4 Work in a group. Find reasons for and against each place on the map in Exercise 3. Then add them to the table.

	positive things	negative things
a near the busy main road		
b in the town		
c on the beach		
d on Green Town Island		

5 In the same group, discuss what you think is the best place for a new café. Compare your answer with a different group. Do you agree? Why / Why not?

REASONS, OPINIONS AND AGREEMENT

1 🔊 6.6 Listen to and read three parts of Listening 2. Notice the underlined phrases. Why do the people use them?

1

Dale: OK, so we need a place for our new office. <u>What about here?</u>

Hakan: Where?

Dale: The city centre. <u>What do you think?</u>

Hakan: Well, <u>it's a good place.</u> <u>It's near some good roads.</u> But ... <u>I don't think we should go there.</u>

Dale: Oh? <u>Why not?</u>

Hakan: <u>Because the buildings in the centre are very old.</u> <u>They are cold in winter and hot in summer, and they're very noisy.</u> <u>They're uncomfortable places.</u>

2

Dale: <u>What about here?</u>

Hakan: The park?

Dale: Yes. <u>It's quiet, and it's not far from a big road.</u> <u>What do you think?</u>

Hakan: Hmm, <u>I'm not sure.</u> <u>It's pretty far from the centre.</u> <u>What about here?</u> Near the train station?

Dale: <u>The train station is good.</u> <u>It's good for travel</u> ... but <u>I think we should go to the park.</u> <u>The buildings near the train station aren't cheap.</u>

3

Hakan: Now <u>what about the design?</u> <u>I think we should have a modern design with big windows.</u> <u>What about you?</u>

Dale: <u>Yes, I agree.</u> <u>Big windows are good.</u>

2 Write the underlined phrases in the correct column of the table.

give a reason	give an opinion	ask for an opinion	agree or disagree

GIVING REASONS

3 Look at the photos of the three cafés again in Exercise 4. Which café would you like to go to? Why? Which café would you not like to go to? Why not? Use the phrases to help you.

I would like to go to ... because ...
Another reason is that ...
Also, it's ... / it's not ...
There is ... there isn't ... / There are ... there aren't ...
I wouldn't like to go to ... because ...

4 Stand up. Ask the questions in Exercise 3 to different students in the class.

Café A

Café B

Café C

GIVING AN OPINION

GRAMMAR

Giving an opinion with *should*

You can give your opinion with the modal *should* + infinitive.

I think we **should** have a small café.
I don't think we **should** have a big café.

5 You are going to open a new school. Write four opinions. Use the phrases in the box to help you.

> have *big / small* classrooms
> have a *modern / traditional* building
> open the school in *a city / the country*
> have *computers / books* in class

I think we should have small classrooms.
1 I think we should _____ .
2 I think we should _____ .
3 I don't think we should _____ .
4 I don't think we should _____ .

ASKING FOR AN OPINION

6 Write the words from the box in the correct gap in the sentences.

> blue   Mexican food   think   you

1 I like modern buildings. What about _____ ?
2 We want to paint the classroom. How about _____ ?
3 I'm going to open a new café. What do you _____ ?
4 Do you want to go to a restaurant this evening? How about _____ ?

AGREEING AND DISAGREEING

7 Do these sentences express agreement (A) or disagreement (D)?

1 I'm not sure.   _____
2 Yes, you're right. _____
3 I don't agree.   _____
4 I agree.   _____

8 Work with a partner. Take turns to be Student A and Student B.

Student A: Give an opinion from Exercise 5 on page 143. Then ask for an opinion.
I think we should have big classrooms. What do you think?
I don't think we should have computers in class. What about you?

Student B: Agree or disagree with Student A.
Yes, I agree.
I'm not sure. I think we should have small classrooms.

PLUS

SPEAKING TASK

You are going to do the speaking task below.

> Discuss ideas for a new café.

PREPARE

1 Look back at your notes in the tables in the Critical thinking section.
Use your notes and the phrases below to prepare for your discussion.

- Where are you going to put your café?

What do you think?	It's near the sea.
What about … ?	There are a lot of hotels here.
I think we should go here.	It's near a busy road.
I think … is the best place.	There are a lot of people in the town.
Why?	Many tourists go on day trips to the island.
Because …	
Yes, I agree.	

- What kind of café is it going to be?

What about … ?	busy
How about … ?	comfortable
I think it should be a …	modern
Yes, I agree.	natural
	quiet
	traditional

- What kind of building is it going to be?

I think we should have …	(a) big (a) small	window(s).		
The walls should be …	metal.	blue.	brown.	
	plastic.	orange.	green.	
The tables and chairs should be …	wooden.	red.	yellow.	
		white.		

2 Read the Task checklist as you prepare for the discussion.

TASK CHECKLIST	✔
Discuss ideas for a café.	
Find reasons for and against.	
Ask for and give opinions.	
Prepare phrases for agreeing and disagreeing.	
Link consonant sounds with vowel sounds.	

DISCUSS

3 Work with a partner. Discuss your ideas for a new café.

Choose ...
- a place.
- a name.
- the design.

4 Tell the class your ideas.

5 Listen to your classmates talk about their ideas. Tell them what you think of their ideas. What are the positive things? What are the negative things?

OBJECTIVES REVIEW

1 Check your learning objectives for this unit. Write *3*, *2* or *1* for each objective.

3 = very well   2 = well   1 = not so well

I can ...

watch and understand a video about a famous house. _____

listen for reasons. _____

evaluate ideas. _____

give reasons. _____

ask for opinions. _____

give an opinion with *should*. _____

agree and disagree. _____

discuss ideas for a new café. _____

2 Go to the *Unlock* Online Workbook for more practice with this unit's learning objectives.

UNLOCK ONLINE

WORDLIST		
armchair (n)	floor (n) ⊙	plastic (adj, n) ⊙
bookcase (n)	furniture (n)	quiet (adj) ⊙
ceiling (n)	glass (adj, n) ⊙	room (n) ⊙
chair (n) ⊙	lamp (n)	sofa (n)
cheap (adj) ⊙	leather (adj, n)	table (n) ⊙
comfortable (adj) ⊙	metal (adj, n) ⊙	uncomfortable (adj)
desk (n)	modern (adj) ⊙	wall (n) ⊙
expensive (adj) ⊙	near (adv, prep) ⊙	wood (n) ⊙
far (adv) ⊙	noisy (adj)	wooden (adj)

⊙ = high-frequency words in the Cambridge Academic Corpus

LEARNING OBJECTIVES	IN THIS UNIT YOU WILL ...
Watch and listen	watch and understand a video about special fruit in Japan.
Listening skill	listen for numbers.
Critical thinking	understand pie charts.
Grammar	use the past simple.
Speaking skills	introduce a report; talk about surveys.
Speaking task	report the results of a survey.

タルトフレーズ
苺のタルト
¥2940 税込
アレルゲン：小麦・卵・乳・ゼラチン

フルーツロー
ふわふわのスポンジに
フレッシュクリームとフル
大 ¥1890 税込

季節限定
桜ケーキ
桜入り
ホワイトチョコレートクリーム
¥420 税込
アレルゲン：小麦・卵・乳・ゼラチン・大豆

フォンダンショコラ
とろけるガナッシュの入った
ガトーショコラ
¥473 税込
アレルゲン：小麦・卵・乳

電子レンジで
２０秒程温めると
より一層美味しく
召し上がれます

フルーツタルト
季節のフルーツ
¥420 税込
アレルゲン：小麦・卵・乳・オレンジ
キウイフルーツ・バナナ・桃・りんご・ゼラチン

シュークリーム
¥263 税込

UNLOCK YOUR KNOWLEDGE

Work with a partner. Ask and answer the questions.

1 What can you see in the photo?
2 Do you often buy things like this?
3 Do people eat things like this in your country?

PLUS

WATCH AND LISTEN

PREPARING TO WATCH

ACTIVATING YOUR KNOWLEDGE

1 Work with a partner and answer the questions.

1 Do you like fruit? What is your favourite kind of fruit?
2 When do most people eat fruit? (for breakfast? after dinner?)
3 What is the most expensive fruit where you live? Why is it so expensive?

PREDICTING
CONTENT
USING VISUALS

2 Look at the pictures from the video. Choose the right word.

1 These *grapes / apples* are very expensive.
2 This box of *vegetables / fruit* looks delicious.
3 The young women are *sitting / standing* in front of a shop.
4 The *farmer / shop manager* is showing the melons.

GLOSSARY

luxury (n) something expensive which is pleasant to have but is not necessary

ordinary (adj) not special at all

taste (v) If food tastes a particular way, it has that flavour in your mouth.

smell (v) to have a quality which people notice by using their noses

care and attention (phr) love and time

dessert (n) a sweet food at the end of a meal

WHILE WATCHING

3 ▶ Watch the video. Tick (✔) the true statements.

☐ 1 You can buy luxury fruit in a supermarket.
☐ 2 Each piece of luxury fruit is the perfect shape and colour.
☐ 3 Luxury fruit is very expensive.
☐ 4 Most people buy luxury fruit for themselves.
☐ 5 Melons are the most expensive luxury fruit in Japan.

4 ▶ Watch again. Circle the correct answers.

1 Luxury fruit is expensive because each one _____ .
   a is a special gift
   b gets a lot of special attention
   c takes a long time to grow

2 The grapes cost _____ .
   a $30
   b $95
   c $175

3 The woman is buying luxury fruit for _____ .
   a her family
   b her boss
   c her husband's parents

4 The woman says luxury fruit _____ .
   a is too expensive
   b is not as good as cake
   c makes people feel happy

5 One pair of melons cost as much as _____ .
   a a car
   b a bicycle
   c a house

5 Complete the sentences with words from the box.

MAKING INFERENCES

| hard   expensive   ordinary   rich |

1 Most people in Japan probably know that a gift of luxury fruit is

   _____ .

2 The person who bought the two expensive melons is probably

   _____ .

3 Growing luxury fruit is probably _____ work.

4 Luxury fruit probably tastes better than _____ fruit.

DISCUSSION

6 Work with a partner and answer the questions.

1 Would you like to try luxury fruit? Which one?
2 Think about luxury fruit as a gift. Who would you buy it for?
3 When you buy a gift for someone special, what do you buy?
4 Do you like gifts you can keep for a long time, or gifts like flowers and fruit that you enjoy for a short time?

LISTENING

LISTENING 1

PREPARING TO LISTEN

USING YOUR
KNOWLEDGE

1 Work with a partner and discuss the questions.

1 What foods are popular in your culture?
2 How often do you eat ...
- Chinese food?
- Mexican food?
- Italian food?
- other kinds of food?

UNDERSTANDING
KEY VOCABULARY

2 You are going to listen to part of a class discussion about food and traditions. Before you listen, read the sentences (1–7). Write the words in bold next to the definitions (a–g).

1 **Meat** was very expensive in the past, but I often eat beef and chicken now.
2 Growing **rice** is hard work, but millions of people eat it every day.
3 Today, in my city, there are many **international** foods. Mexican, Chinese and Italian foods are very popular.
4 We eat a lot of **fish**. We live near water.
5 My grandmother makes many special **dishes**. She cooks all day to prepare them.
6 Salad is made of **vegetables**. It's very good for you. It's fresh and is usually green.
7 I don't have time to cook dinner every night, so sometimes I eat **fast food**. But I know it's bad for me.

a _____ (n) food which is prepared in a special way and given a name
b _____ (n) parts of animals used as food
c _____ (n) small, white or brown grains from a plant which are cooked and eaten
d _____ (n) food which is served very quickly in a restaurant because it is already prepared
e _____ (n) plants which are used as food
f _____ (adj) from more than one country
g _____ (n) an animal which lives in water and swims using its tail and fins

SKILLS

Numbers with -teen and -ty

🔊 7.1 In English, it is often difficult to hear the difference between 'teen numbers (e.g. 13, 14, 15) and 'ty numbers (e.g. 30, 40, 50).

For -teen numbers:

- stress the first syllable when the number is before a noun.
  Fif-teen thousand pounds every month?
  Se-ven-teen million?

- stress the last syllable when the number is at the end of a statement.
  Sorry – how many children? Six-teen?

For -ty numbers, always stress the first syllable.
We feed six-ty children from poor families here. Fif-ty? No, six-ty.
Listen to how the examples above are pronounced.

3 🔊 7.2 Listen to and read these conversations. Circle the numbers you hear.

1 A: Is the number of people there about *17 / 70* million?
   B: Er, no, I think it's about *17 / 70*.
   A: *Seventeen / Seventy* million? OK, thanks.

2 A: We feed *16 / 60* children from poor families here.
   B: Sorry – how many children? *Sixteen / sixty*?
   A: No, *16 / 60*.

3 A: *Thirteen / Thirty* percent of this class are vegetarians – people who don't eat meat.
   B: *Thirteen / Thirty*? Are you sure?
   A: No, no – *13 / 30*!

4 A: People in this city eat *15 / 50* thousand tonnes of beef every month.
   B: Is that true? *Fifteen / Fifty* thousand tonnes every month?
   A: No, *15 / 50* thousand – not *15 / 50*.

WHILE LISTENING

LISTENING FOR
MAIN IDEAS

GLOSSARY

traditional (adj) doing things the way that people have done them for a long time

4 🔊 7.3 Listen to a class discussion. What is the main topic of the class discussion? Choose the correct answer.

a how our grandparents cooked traditional foods
b how more international foods are changing the way we eat
c how international foods are good for you

5 🔊 7.3 Listen again. Write *T* (true) or *F* (false) for each statement. Correct the false statements.

_____ 1 The average person in the UK eats meat three times a day.
_____ 2 Yuki's grandparents ate fish.
_____ 3 José's grandmother cooked traditional dishes.
_____ 4 International foods are available in José's country.
_____ 5 Most of the students know how to cook traditional dishes.

Listening for numbers

You often hear facts in class discussions. Many facts are about numbers.

There are **40** students in the class.
In Argentina, **97%** of the people can read and write.

6 🔊 7.3 Listen again. Write the number you hear next to each phrase.

1 _____ years ago = how long ago José's grandmother cooked traditional food every day
2 _____ = the number of students who can cook
3 _____ percent = the number of students who can cook traditional foods

7 Work with a partner. Compare answers. Use the phrases to help you.

What do you have for number ... ?

I have ...

What about you?

I don't know the answer.

DISCUSSION

8 Work in groups. Discuss the questions.

1 What foods did your family eat when you were a child? Do you eat the same foods now, or different ones?
2 Do you think it's important to know how to cook traditional food? Why / Why not?
3 Are there some foods people in your country do not eat? What is the reason?

THE PAST SIMPLE 1

GRAMMAR

Statements

Use the past simple to talk about an event or an activity in the past.

Add -ed to most regular verbs in the past. Add -d to verbs which end in -e.

subject	verb + -ed or -d
I / He / She / You / We / They	cooked dinner last night. lived in Japan five years ago.

My grandmother **cooked** traditional dishes.

We **lived** in a big city 10 years ago.

Add did + not / didn't before the infinitive in the negative.

subject	did not / didn't + infinitive
I / He / She / You / We / They	**did not cook** traditional dishes. **didn't cook** traditional dishes.

My grandmother **didn't cook** traditional dishes.

We **didn't live** in a big city 10 years ago.

1 Write the verbs in brackets in the past simple.

1 We _____ (live) in Mexico 10 years ago.

2 My mum _____ (cook) Italian food a lot.

3 I _____ (not cook) last night.

4 My grandfather _____ (work) in a restaurant.

5 My grandparents _____ (live) by the water.

6 My sister and I _____ (watch) my grandmother cook.

7 We _____ (not help) her cook.

8 My grandfather _____ (not learn) to cook.

Yes/No questions and short answers

Use *did* or *didn't* + subject + the infinitive to form questions in the past simple.

did / didn't	subject	infinitive
Did	I / he / she / you / we / they	**eat** dinner last night?

Short answers:
Yes, I / he / she / you / we / they **did**.
No, I / he / she / you / we / they **didn't**.

2 Answer the questions so they are true for you.

1 When you were a child, did you live in a big city?
   <u>No, I didn't live in a big city. I lived in a small town.</u>

2 Did both of your parents work?
   _____

3 Did your grandmother cook traditional dishes?
   _____

4 Did you celebrate holidays with special foods?
   _____

5 Did your family talk a lot at the dinner table?
   _____

6 Did you watch TV during dinner?
   _____

3 Write the questions in the past simple. Then work with a partner and ask and answer the questions.

1 you / have a traditional meal last night?
   <u>Did you have a traditional meal last night?</u>

2 you / eat at a fast food restaurant this week?
   _____

3 you / cook dinner last week?
   _____

4 you / eat a big lunch yesterday?
   _____

5 you / eat breakfast today?
   _____

6 you / have a meal with friends last week?
   _____

4 Work with a new partner. Ask and answer the questions in Exercise 3 about your previous partner.

A: Did Yara have a traditional meal last night?
B: No, she didn't.

Irregular verbs

Some verbs are irregular. They do not add -d / -ed in the past simple.

be → was / were	go → went
buy → bought	have → had
come → came	make → made
do → did	read → read
eat → ate	

I **made** a special dish from my country last week.
I **ate** something new last night.
This vegetable **came** from Mexico.

Remember: Use the infinitive after *didn't* in the negative.
I **didn't eat** dinner last night.

5 Write the verbs in brackets in the past simple.

1 No, I _____ (not make) special dishes for the party.
2 He _____ (eat) a lot of fish in Japan.
3 She _____ (buy) a lot of food at the supermarket.
4 No, it _____ (be) too expensive, so people didn't eat it very much.
5 No, she _____ (not do) any cooking when she was visiting her family.
6 This fruit _____ (come) from Japan.
7 We _____ (not have) time to cook last night, so we _____ (go) to a restaurant.
8 I _____ (read) an interesting cookbook about Mexican food last night.

6 Write true sentences about you. Use the past simple of the verbs in brackets. Then read your sentences to a partner.

1 Last week, I _____ (make).
2 Last night, I _____ (have) _____ for dinner.
3 Yesterday, I _____ (eat) _____ for breakfast.
4 Last month, I _____ (buy).
5 Last year, my family _____ (go).
6 Last week, I _____ (read).

7 Correct the mistakes in the sentences.

1 I eated a big breakfast this morning.
2 Did you had fish for dinner last week?
3 They didn't cooked dinner for their family last Sunday.
4 I learnd to cook from my father.
5 Did Kevin makes dinner last night?
6 We wented to a great new restaurant on Friday.
7 Emma didn't not liked her meal.
8 Had you lunch with your parents yesterday?

PLUS

VOCABULARY FOR FOOD

8 Look at the photos of different kinds of food. Add as many other foods to the table as you can.

meat	vegetables	other

9 Work with a partner. Are the photos of fast food (*F*), traditional food (*T*) or healthy food (*H*)? Write *F*, *T* or *H* under the photos. More than one letter is possible.

sandwich   noodles   pizza   salad

1 _____   2 _____   3 _____   4 _____

tacos   chips   burger   pasta

5 _____   6 _____   7 _____   8 _____

10 How many students in the class like each kind of food? Stand up and ask and answer questions. Use the phrases from the box to help you.

questions	Do you like … ?
	What about … ?
	What food don't you like?
	What food do you like best?
	Is this a traditional food in your country? Which foods do you use to make a traditional dish in your country?
answers	I like … because … I don't like … because …
	The food I like is …
	Yes / No …
	In my country, we use … to make …

LISTENING 2

PREPARING TO LISTEN

UNDERSTANDING KEY VOCABULARY

1 Write the words from the box in the correct gap in the sentences below.

> **culture** (n) the usual way of living in a country or for a group of people
> **enjoy** (v) to get pleasure from something
> **favourite** (adj) your favourite person or thing is the one you like best
> **healthy** (adj) good for your health
> **home-cooked** (adj) when food is cooked at home
> **meal** (n) the food which you eat at breakfast, lunch or dinner

1 My grandmother almost never ate at restaurants. She always made good food at home. Everyone liked her _____ food.
2 Which _____ do you like best – breakfast, lunch or dinner?
3 Eating out is not always _____ . It's probably better to cook fresh food at home.
4 My _____ food is Italian.
5 I really _____ going to restaurants which serve international food. It's always fun to try something new.
6 In my country's _____ , we usually make special meals for celebrations and holidays.

2 You are going to hear a student giving a report. Before you listen, look at the information below. Discuss the questions with a partner.

1 What kind of restaurant are you going to hear about in Question 1?

2 Which answer do you think will be more popular to Question 2: 'Yes' or 'No'?

3 What do you think the answer will be in Question 3?

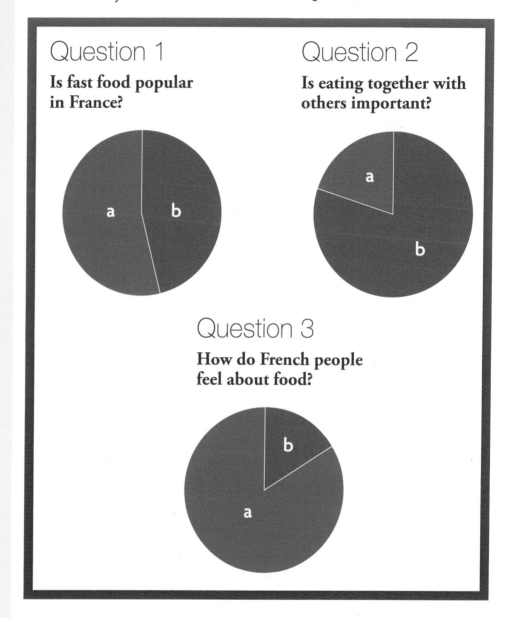

Question 1

Is fast food popular in France?

Question 2

Is eating together with others important?

Question 3

How do French people feel about food?

WHILE LISTENING

3 🔊 **7.4** Listen to a student reporting the results of a survey. Choose the
correct answers.

LISTENING FOR
MAIN IDEAS

1 The main topic of her survey is ...
   a food from around the world.
   b food and culture in one country.
   c family meals.
2 Most people eat meals ...
   a alone.
   b at work.
   c with others.
3 The student thinks that fast food ...
   a is not popular.
   b is changing the way people eat in France.
   c tastes bad in France.

4 🔊 **7.4** Listen again. Write *T* (true) or *F* (false) for each statement.
Correct the false statements.

LISTENING
FOR DETAIL

_____ 1 Fifty-four percent of all restaurant sales were from fast
food places.

_____

_____ 2 Eighty percent of people like to eat with others.

_____

_____ 3 In France, enjoying food is very important.

_____

_____ 4 Because of the French culture, fast food restaurants have to
cook better meals than usual.

_____

_____ 5 Traditions about eating are the same now as they were before.

_____

DISCUSSION

5 Work with a partner. Think about the information from Listening 1
and Listening 2 and discuss the questions.

SYNTHESIZING

1 How do people feel about food in your country?
2 Is fast food more popular than home-cooked meals in your country?

SPEAKING

CRITICAL THINKING

At the end of this unit, you are going to do the speaking task below.

▶ Report the results of a survey.

SKILLS

Understanding pie charts

The diagrams in Listening 2 on page 160 and below are pie charts. We can use pie charts to show results from a survey in a different way from just numbers. Pie charts use percentages (%).

 APPLY

1 🔊 7.4 Look at the pie charts on page 160. Listen and label parts a and b in the charts with words from the box. Then check your answers with a partner.

> fast food sales / sales from other restaurants
> eating together is important / eating together is not important
> enjoy food / don't enjoy food

 UNDERSTAND

2 Work in two groups, A and B. Look at the information in your pie charts.

Group A: Changes in food and culture – country A

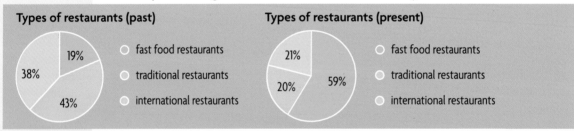

Types of restaurants (past)
19%
38%
43%
○ fast food restaurants
○ traditional restaurants
○ international restaurants

Types of restaurants (present)
21%
20%
59%
○ fast food restaurants
○ traditional restaurants
○ international restaurants

Eating habits (past)
35%
65%
● eating alone
● eating together

Eating habits (present)
25%
75%
● eating alone
● eating together

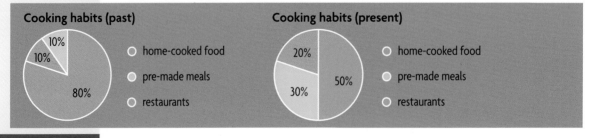

Cooking habits (past)
10%
10%
80%
○ home-cooked food
○ pre-made meals
○ restaurants

Cooking habits (present)
20%
30%
50%
○ home-cooked food
○ pre-made meals
○ restaurants

Group B: Changes in food and culture – country B

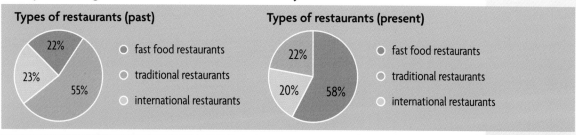

Types of restaurants (past)

- fast food restaurants
- traditional restaurants
- international restaurants

22%
23%
55%

Types of restaurants (present)

- fast food restaurants
- traditional restaurants
- international restaurants

22%
20%
58%

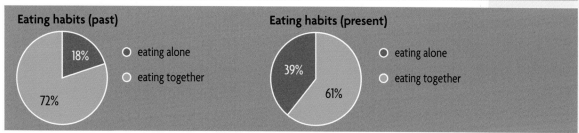

Eating habits (past)

- eating alone
- eating together

18%
72%

Eating habits (present)

- eating alone
- eating together

39%
61%

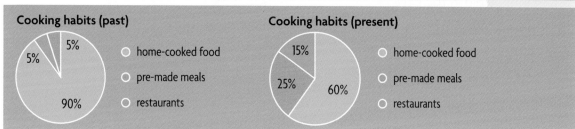

Cooking habits (past)

- home-cooked food
- pre-made meals
- restaurants

5%
5%
90%

Cooking habits (present)

- home-cooked food
- pre-made meals
- restaurants

15%
25%
60%

3 Work in your groups and answer the questions.

ANALYZE

1 What information does each pie chart show?

_____

_____

2 What do you think the three survey questions were?

_____

_____

3 Are fast food restaurants more popular now?

_____

_____

4 Do families eat together more than before?

_____

_____

5 Do people eat the same food as they did in the past?

_____

_____

6 What food do people eat now?

_____

_____

4 Look at the reasons in the box below. Match the reasons to the results in the table. More than one answer may be possible.

result	reason for result
1 In the past, there were more international and traditional restaurants.	
2 Now there are more fast food restaurants.	
3 In the past, people usually ate together.	
4 Now, people eat alone more often than they did in the past.	
5 In the past, people usually ate home-cooked foods.	
6 Now, people often eat pre-made foods or eat at restaurants.	

Reasons

People eat smaller lunches, such as fast food, which don't take as long.

Families are not together because of working hours.

Families eat at popular fast food restaurants as a special occasion.

Families ate big lunches together.

More food is available from around the world.

Fast food is cheap and easy.

People don't know how to cook.

Pre-made meals are available at supermarkets.

Traditional restaurants are more expensive.

International food or international restaurants are more popular.

Fast food was not available.

People couldn't buy food from other countries.

People don't have time to cook.

5 Think of other reasons for the results in the pie charts and add them to the table in Exercise 4. Use Listening 1 and Listening 2 to help you.

INTRODUCING A REPORT

1 🔊 7.5 Sophie uses six statements to introduce her report. Number the statements in the correct order. Then listen and check.

_____ **a** My questions were on the topic of food and culture in France.

_____ **b** This afternoon, I'm going to tell you about the results of my survey.

_____ **c** There were three questions in my survey.

_____ **d** I'm Sophie.

_____ **e** I think this is an interesting topic.

_____ **f** Hello!

2 🔊 7.6 Listen to two more introductions. Write the words from the box in the gaps (1–8).

> three   five   everybody   fast   good
> interesting   morning   traditional

Good (1)_____ ! I'm Tomoko. I'm going to tell you about the results of my survey. There were (2)_____ questions in my survey. My topic was (3)_____ Japanese food. I think this is an (4)_____ topic.

Hello, (5)_____ ! I'm Ahmed. I'm going to tell you about the results of my survey. My topic was (6)_____ food in Jeddah. There were (7)_____ questions in my survey. I think this is a (8)_____ topic.

SKILLS

The letter *u*

The letter *u* is pronounced in different ways. Look at the words with different *u* sounds.

> question   survey   result   UK   popular

3 🔊 7.7 Listen to the different *u* sounds in the words in the box above. Then listen again and repeat.

4 🔊 7.8 Listen to the sentences. Notice the way we pronounce the *u* sound in the underlined words. Listen again and repeat.

1 I'm going to tell you about the <u>results</u> of my <u>survey</u>.
2 There were <u>four</u> <u>questions</u> about food and <u>culture</u>.
3 Are fast food restaurants <u>popular</u>?
4 People had 80 <u>minutes</u> for <u>lunch</u>.

TALKING ABOUT SURVEYS

5 Read the phrases from six statements from Sophie's report.

a My last question was
b My second question was
c So, when you look here
d In one survey I read
e You can see here that
f my first question was

6 🔊 7.9 Write the correct phrases (a–f) in the gaps. Listen and check.

1 So, _____ , 'Is fast food popular in France?'
2 _____ 54% percent of all restaurant sales were from fast food places.
3 _____ , in the past, people had 80 minutes for lunch, but now only 22 minutes.
4 _____ 'Is eating together with others important?'
5 _____ , 'How do French people feel about food?'
6 _____ , 84% of the people in France enjoy food.

7 Work with a partner. Take turns to report on the survey questions about food and culture in country A and country B from the Critical thinking section. Use the phrases in Exercise 5 to talk about the pie charts.

> My first question was, 'Are fast food restaurants popular now?'
> You can see here that the answer is 'yes'. In the past,
> _____ % of all restaurants were fast food restaurants.
> Now, _____ % of the restaurants are fast food restaurants.

📱 PLUS

SPEAKING TASK

▶ Report the results of a survey.

PREPARE

1 Work with a partner. One student is from Group A (country A) in the Critical thinking section. The other student is from Group B (country B).

2 Review the results of the survey about country A or country B and your answers to the questions in the Critical thinking section. Remember to give reasons for your answers.

3 Prepare an introduction for your report.

> Hello, _____ ! I'm _____ .
> I'm going to tell you about the results of a survey. The topic
> was _____ in (country A / B). There were
> _____ questions in the survey. I think this is a / an
> _____ topic.

4 Read the Task checklist as you prepare your report.

TASK CHECKLIST	✔
Report the results of the survey about country A or B.	
Use your answers and reasons to the three survey questions in your report.	
Introduce your report.	
Use the pie charts in your report.	
Use the correct stress and -teen / -ty pronunciation for numbers. Use the correct pronunciation for the u sound.	

DISCUSS

5 Talk about the results from the survey about your country. Use your notes from the Critical thinking section. Practise your introduction.

6 Change partners and report the results of your survey.

OBJECTIVES REVIEW

1 Check your learning objectives for this unit. Write *3, 2* or *1* for each objective.

   3 = very well   2 = well   1 = not so well

   I can ...

   watch and understand a video about special fruit in Japan.   _____

   listen for numbers.   _____

   understand pie charts.   _____

   use the past simple.   _____

   introduce a report.   _____

   talk about surveys.   _____

   report the results of a survey.   _____

2 Go to the *Unlock* Online Workbook for more practice with this unit's learning objectives.

UNLOCK
ONLINE

WORDLIST		
burger (n)	fish (n) ⊙	pasta (n)
chips (n)	healthy (adj) ⊙	pizza (n)
culture (n) ⊙	home-cooked (adj)	rice (n) ⊙
dish (n)	international (adj) ⊙	salad (n)
enjoy (v) ⊙	meal (n)	sandwich (n)
fast food (n)	meat (n) ⊙	tacos (n)
favourite (adj)	noodles (n)	vegetable (n)

⊙ = high-frequency words in the Cambridge Academic Corpus

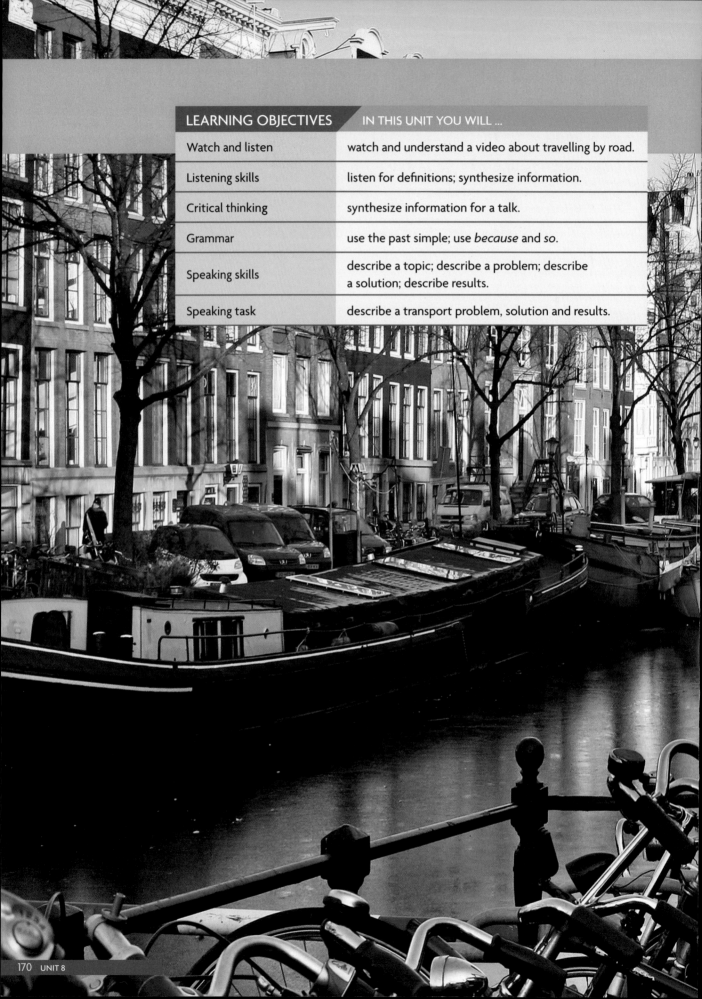

LEARNING OBJECTIVES	IN THIS UNIT YOU WILL ...
Watch and listen	watch and understand a video about travelling by road.
Listening skills	listen for definitions; synthesize information.
Critical thinking	synthesize information for a talk.
Grammar	use the past simple; use *because* and *so*.
Speaking skills	describe a topic; describe a problem; describe a solution; describe results.
Speaking task	describe a transport problem, solution and results.

TRANSPORT

UNL○CK YOUR KNOWLEDGE

Work with a partner. Ask and answer the questions.

1 Look at the photo. Which country do you think this is? Why?

2 Which forms of transport in the photo ...

  a are more modern?

  b did people use in the past?

3 Do you think this city has a problem with transport?

PLUS

PREPARING TO WATCH

ACTIVATING YOUR
KNOWLEDGE

1 Work with a partner. Discuss the questions.

1 How do you get to school?
2 Are the roads busy? Is there a lot of traffic?
3 Are the roads big and wide or small and narrow in your town or city?

PREDICTING
CONTENT USING
VISUALS

2 Look at the pictures from the video. Put the words in order to make sentences.

1 many roads / has / The / city / .

_____

2 not much traffic / There is / in / the country / .

_____

3 The road / the mountain / goes / under / .

_____

4 bridge / long / between / There / a / is / mountains / the / .

_____

GLOSSARY

amazing (adj) very surprising

connect (v) to join two things together

construct (v) to build, for example, houses or roads

highway (n) a main, usually large, road

port (n) an area of a town next to water where ships arrive and leave

WHILE WATCHING

3 ▶ Watch the video. Write *T* (true) or *F* (false) next to the statements. Correct the false statements.

_____ 1 More people travel on roads today.

_____

_____ 2 The largest builder of roads is the United States.

_____

_____ 3 China has 47,000 miles of highways.

_____

_____ 4 The G50 connects the middle of China to Shanghai.

_____

_____ 5 The Sidu Bridge is not the world's highest bridge.

_____

4 ▶ Watch again. Put the sentences in the order that you hear the information.

_____ In 1989, China had fewer than 100 miles of highway.
_____ The G50 goes through mountains and includes the highest bridge.
_____ The G50 is almost 1,200 miles long.
_____ The number of roads is growing all the time.
_____ China has more highways than the United States.

5 Choose the correct answers. Compare your answers with a partner.

1 Why does China need more roads?
   a There are more people visiting China.
   b The number of cars is growing.
   c There are many old roads.
2 Why is it important to connect the middle of China to the port city of Shanghai?
   a People in the middle of China don't have to travel to Shanghai.
   b People like to visit the east coast.
   c People in the middle of China can easily send and receive more things.

DISCUSSION

6 Work with a partner. Discuss the questions.

1 Is your city or country building more roads every year? Why / Why not?
2 What important places do the main roads in your country connect?
3 Is there a road similar to the G50 in your country? What is it?
4 Do you think the G50 is amazing? Why / Why not?

LISTENING

LISTENING 1

PREPARING TO LISTEN

UNDERSTANDING
KEY VOCABULARY

1 Write the words from the box in the correct gap in the sentences below.

> **bus** (n) a big vehicle which takes many people around a city
> **journey** (n) travelling from one place to another in a car, bus, train, the metro, etc.
> **metro** (n) trains which travel underground in a city (In London, people call the metro the 'Underground'.)
> **passenger** (n) someone who travels in a car, bus, etc., but doesn't drive it
> **taxi** (n) a car with a driver who you pay to take you somewhere
> **ticket** (n) a small piece of paper which shows you paid to do something
> **train** (n) a long, thin type of car which travels on metal tracks and carries people or things
> **travel** (v) to go from one place to another, usually over a long distance

1 I go to work by train and I really enjoy the _____ because I find time to read.
2 My children take the _____ to school every day. It stops on our street. The driver is very nice and knows everyone's name.
3 I'm sorry, but there is no public transport here. I can call a _____ to take you to the airport from your hotel. It will cost about £60.
4 The _____ is one of the best in the world. It's fast and easy to use. Millions of people use it every day.
5 When I was in Europe, I rode on the _____ from city to city. It was a great way to see the countryside and small towns.
6 There was a nice _____ who gave me his seat because it was the only one free.
7 Excuse me. I would like to go to Hanover Station. How much is a one-way _____ , please?
8 In many cities, people _____ many kilometres to work.

2 Work with a partner. Discuss the questions.

1 What do you know about London?

2 How do you think people travel to work and school in London?

3 Circle the correct answers.

1 Excuse me! How much is a train *passenger / ticket* to Liverpool?

2 Hi! How was your *journey / passenger* to London?

3 I had a conversation with an interesting *passenger / ticket* on the train.

4 You are going to listen to a man named Steve Miller talk about transport for London. Before you listen, decide if the types of transport in the box are private (only for the person who owns it) or public (for everyone to use). Write them in the correct column of the table.

bus car metro taxi train

private	public

5 Which of these types of transport in London do you think are …

a the easiest?

b the cheapest?

c the most expensive?

PRONUNCIATION FOR LISTENING

SKILLS

Pronouncing years

1994   [nineteen] [ninety-four]

1238   [twelve] [thirty-eight]

570   [five hundred] and [seventy]

2005   [two thousand] and [five]

2017   [two thousand] and [seventeen] / [twenty seventeen]

6 🔊 8.1 Look at the years. Listen and repeat.

| 1238 | 1868 | 1923 | 1996 | 2005 |

7 🔊 8.2 Listen and write the years.

1 _____   4 _____

2 _____   5 _____

3 _____

8 How is the last number in Exercise 7 different?

> **GLOSSARY**
>
> **result** (n) something which happens because something else has happened

9 Work with a partner. What can you see in the photos?

a

the London Underground – the world's oldest metro system

b

Steve Miller works for Transport for London.

c

There are many people who travel in London.

d

Many Londoners use an electronic ticket, the Oyster card.

e

an electronic gate from the London Underground

WHILE LISTENING

10 🔊 8.3 Listen to Steve Miller talk about Transport for London and take notes.

Topic: (1)_____

Transport for London: (2)_____

_____

People travelling in London: (3)_____

_____

London Underground opened: (4)_____

Oyster card: (5)_____

_____

11 Work with a partner. Use your notes to answer the questions.

1 What is the topic of Steve's talk?

2 What does Transport for London (TfL) do?

3 How many people travel in London?

4 What's the age of the London Underground?

5 What is an Oyster card?

12 🔊 8.3 Listen again and answer the questions.

1 Which five forms of transport does Steve talk about?

- London Underground

- _____

- _____

- _____

- _____

2 What year did TfL introduce Oyster cards?

3 Why did TfL need Oyster cards?

4 What are three newer ways to pay for tickets?

DISCUSSION

13 Work with a partner. Ask and answer the questions.

1 Do you live in a busy city? If not, have you visited one? Do / Did you like it?

2 Which types of transport do you use? What do you use them for?

3 Which type of transport do you use most often? Why?

VERBS FOR TRANSPORT

take a bus, train, taxi, ferry, the metro

bus

train

ferry

metro

taxi

drive a car

car

go by bus, train, metro, taxi, car, ferry

bus

train

car

metro

taxi

ferry

ride a bike / **cycle**

bike / bicycle

ride a motorbike

motorbike

go on foot

foot

1 Write the correct form of the verbs. Use the table with verbs for transport on page 178 to help you.

1 Can you _____ the metro to the supermarket in your hometown?
2 Do you like to _____ by train or by bus?
3 Do you know how to _____ a car?
4 Where do you _____ on foot?

PLUS

2 Answer the questions in Exercise 1 so they are true for you. Then work with a partner and practise asking and answering the questions. Give reasons for your answers.

1 Yes, I can take the metro. / No, I can't take the metro.

THE PAST SIMPLE 2

GRAMMAR

More irregular verbs

Use the past simple to talk about an event or activity in the past.
There are many irregular past tense verbs. They do not add -d / -ed in the past simple. You learned some irregular past tense forms in Unit 7. Here are more irregular verbs in the past simple.

drive → **drove**   sit → **sat**
go → **went**   take → **took**
run → **ran**

3 Circle the correct past simple verb form.

1 I *sitted / sat* near the front of the bus.
2 Harvey *taked / took* the ferry to work yesterday.
3 We *went / goes* to the restaurant by taxi.
4 Akito *drove / drived* his new car to the cinema last night.
5 They *runs / ran* five kilometres after work.

4 Write the verbs in brackets in the past simple.

1 It was raining. She _____ (take) a taxi.
2 He _____ (run) to the train station.
3 She _____ (sit) by the window.
4 She _____ (drive) to her friend's house.
5 She _____ (go) by bus.

BECAUSE / SO

Use *because* and *so* to show reasons that something happened or the result of something. *Because* and *so* are followed by a subject and verb.

Because + subject and verb: to show a reason.
So + subject and verb: to show a result.

I took the train **because** it was faster. (reason: because it was faster)
It was a beautiful day, **so** I rode my bicycle. (result: so I rode my bicycle)
Amber rode her bike to work **because** she wanted to get exercise.
(reason: because she wanted to get exercise)
Sam missed the bus, so he drove to work. (result: so he drove to work)

5 Match the sentences (1–5) from Exercise 4 to the reasons and results using *because* and *so*. Then write the complete sentences.

_____ **a** ... because he was late.
   He ran to the train station because he was late.

_____ **b** ... because it was too far to walk.

   _____

_____ **c** ... so she had a view of the beautiful countryside.

   _____

_____ **d** ... so she didn't get wet from the rain.

   _____

_____ **e** ... because there was a bus station near the house.

   _____

PLUS

6 Write information which is true for you. Then read your sentences to a partner.

1 I like to go on foot because ... / I don't like to go on foot because ...
2 I cycle because ... / I don't cycle because ...
3 I like to go by train, so ... / I don't like to go by train, so ...
4 Petrol is expensive, so ... / Petrol isn't expensive, so ...

LISTENING 2

PREPARING TO LISTEN

USING YOUR KNOWLEDGE

1 You are going to listen to someone describing a solution to a transport problem. Before you listen, look at the pictures and discuss the questions with a partner.

traffic   moving walkway   car sharing   pollution   self-driving car

  1 Which of these things in the pictures do you have in your country?

  2 How do you feel about what you see in the pictures?

UNDERSTANDING KEY VOCABULARY

2 Write the words from the box in the correct gap in the sentences below.

> **accident** (n) a bad situation that is not expected and which causes pain or problems
> **idea** (n) a suggestion or plan for doing something
> **pavement** (n) a hard path for people to walk on next to a road
> **petrol** (n) what most cars need in order to move
> **problem** (n) something which makes life difficult and needs a solution
> **traffic** (n) the cars and other vehicles driving on the road

1 The city planners had a new _____ to make travel times shorter for people.

2 There are too many cars and trucks on the road. The _____ is very bad today!

3 Oh, dear. I have to put more _____ in my car before I go to work. It's so expensive!

4 We need more roads or buses or metro lines. It's a big _____ in many big cities.

5 There was an _____ on this road last night and people were hurt.

6 It's too hot outside in this city, so people don't like to walk on the _____ .

PLUS

PRONUNCIATION FOR LISTENING

SKILLS

Consonant clusters

A consonant cluster is a group of consonants. Some consonant clusters have a special sound. Here are some examples. The consonant clusters are in bold.

what ('wh' sounds like 'w')

quick ('ck' sounds like 'k')

phone ('ph' sounds like 'f')

tough ('gh' sometimes sounds like 'f')

moving

3 🔊 8.4 Listen and repeat the sentences.

1 Cycling is sometimes quicker than driving.
2 You shouldn't talk on your phone when you're driving.
3 Driving when there's a lot of traffic is tough.
4 I don't have enough money to buy a car.
5 What kind of ticket should I buy?

4 Work with a partner. Practise saying the sentences in Exercise 3.

WHILE LISTENING

SKILLS

Listening for definitions

Good speakers explain the meaning of new or difficult words. They give a definition of the words. We can use the words and phrases in bold to define key vocabulary.

A self-driving car **is a kind of** car that drives without a driver.
It's a self-driving car. **That means** it doesn't need a driver.
A moving walkway **means** a pavement that moves people.
It's a moving walkway, **so** people walk faster on it.

5 🔊 8.5 Listen to the first part of a talk about transport problems and solutions. Work with a partner. What do the words in bold mean?

1 Many cities often have **gridlock** on the streets. That means …
2 **Smog** is a kind of …
3 They have **bicycle-sharing** programmes, so …
4 **Car sharing** means …

6 🔊 8.5 Listen again and take notes. Then compare your notes with a partner.

Topic: _Transport in cities: Problems and solutions_

Problems:

Cities have a lot of (1)_____ problems. Many people use their
(2)_____ .

It takes more (3)_____ and (4)_____ to
travel around the city.

This is (5)_____ for people and the (6)_____
is very bad.

Solutions:

Some cities think that (7)_____ are a good idea.

Other cities have (8)_____ .

There's another new (9)_____ that is interesting.

It's a (10)_____ car!

It can help stop (11)_____ .

7 🔊 8.6 Listen to the second part of the talk. What are two transport problems in Dubai? What are the solutions and their results? Take notes, and then compare your notes with a partner.

Dubai

Problem:

(1)_____

Solution:

(2)_____

Result:

(3)_____

Problem:

(4)_____

_____

Solution:

(5)_____

Results:

(6)_____

_____

8 Answer the questions. Use your notes to help you.

1 Why do cities have traffic problems?
2 What are some problems with cars?
3 What do some cities think are good ideas?
4 Which place is working hard to improve their traffic problems?
5 What is the plan in this place?

DISCUSSION

Synthesizing information

When you *synthesize information*, you think about the connection between more than one source (e.g. a text or a listening). For example, you can read about an idea in a text and then watch a video which has a good example of this idea. Synthesizing information helps you to understand problems, explain results or find solutions.

9 Work with a partner. Discuss the questions. Use the information from Listening 1 and Listening 2 to help you.

1 In Listening 1, you hear about the London Underground. In Listening 2, Dubai plans to build a metro system like London's. Do you think people in Dubai will use the metro as much as people do in London? Why / Why not?

2 How are transport problems the same in London and Dubai? How are they different?

3 In Dubai, moving walkways are a solution to a transport problem. Do you think there should be moving walkways in London? Why / Why not? What are some other cities where moving walkways would help?

SYNTHESIZING

SPEAKING

CRITICAL THINKING

At the end of this unit, you are going to do the Speaking task below.

> Describe a transport problem, solutions and results.

1 Write down the transport problems, solutions and results you heard in Listening 1 and Listening 2 in the table. Use your notes to help you. Then check your answers with a partner and add any missing information.

problem	solution	result
paper tickets very slow	Oyster cards / credit cards / mobile phone payments	pay online / walk through gates faster

2 Work in two groups.

Group A: Go to page 193 and read about the transport problems, their solutions and the results in the Santa Fe district of Mexico City, Mexico. Then answer the questions.

Group B: Go to page 195 and read about the transport problems, their solutions and the results in Melbourne, Australia. Then answer the questions.

 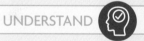

SKILLS

Synthesizing information for a talk

When you prepare a talk, try to make it interesting. Synthesizing information from different sources (like here, with the two listenings) is a good way to do this.

3 **Group A:** Create a table like the one below. Write your answers from page 193 in the table. Add your own ideas for solutions and results, and add ideas from Listenings 1 and 2.

Group B: Create a table like the one below. Write your answers from page 195 in the table. Add your own ideas for solutions and results, and add ideas from Listenings 1 and 2.

city: _____	topic: _____	
problem	**solution**	**result**

 EVALUATE

4 Look at all the results in the table above. Which solution do you think is the most effective? Why? Work with a partner and give your reasons.

PREPARATION FOR SPEAKING

DESCRIBING A TOPIC

1 🔊 8.7 Listen to Iman again. Then write the words and phrases from the box in the gaps.

> because   More and more   This is   This means   With all of

(1)_____ people are living in cities rather than in the countryside. (2)_____ that cities have a lot of traffic problems (3)_____ many people use their cars to go to work or school or shop ... or whatever. Many cities often have gridlock on the streets. This means the cars can't move. (4)_____ these cars, it takes more time and petrol to travel around the city. (5)_____ expensive for people. Also, the smog is very bad in some places.

DESCRIBING A PROBLEM

2 🔊 8.8 Write the verbs in brackets in the past simple. Then listen to Steve Miller and check your answers.

Each passenger (1)_____ (wait) to buy a ticket and then they (2)_____ (go) to the gate. At the gate, they (3)_____ (put) the ticket into the machine. Then the gate (4)_____ (open) and then they (5)_____ (take) their ticket from the machine. Now, this (6)_____ (take) a long time, and more people (7)_____ (start) to live and work in London, so we (8)_____ (need) a faster ticket system. And this (9)_____ (be) the Oyster card.

3 Which verbs in Exercise 2 are irregular past simple verbs?

PRONUNCIATION FOR SPEAKING

-d / -ed in regular past simple verbs

There are three ways to pronounce the *-d* and *-ed* endings of regular verbs in the past simple.

When a verb ends in these sounds, *-ed* is pronounced as /t/:	When a verb ends with a vowel sound or these consonant sounds, *-ed* is pronounced as /d/:	When a regular verb ends with a /t/ or /d/ sound, *-ed* is pronounced as /ɪd/:
sto**p** /p/	gra**b** /b/	visi**t** /t/
lau**gh** /f/	jo**g** /g/	deci**de** /d/
mi**ss** /s/	sa**ve** /v/	
li**ke** /k/	bu**zz** /z/	
fini**sh** /ʃ/	massa**ge** /ʒ/	
wa**tch** /tʃ/	chan**ge** /dʒ/	
	clim**b** /m/	
	liste**n** /n/	
	trave**l** /l/	
	brea**the** /ð/	

SKILLS

4 🔊 8.9 Listen and repeat the verbs in the past simple.

happened _____	needed _____	showed _____
changed _____	waited _____	watched _____
visited _____	asked _____	opened _____
guessed _____	helped _____	started _____

5 🔊 8.9 Listen again. What sound do you hear at the end of each verb? Write /t/, /d/ or /ɪd/ next to each verb in Exercise 4.

6 Choose five verbs from the box above. Write a true sentence about you with the past simple form of each verb.

1 _____

2 _____

3 _____

4 _____

5 _____

7 Read your sentences from Exercise 6 to a partner. Listen to your partner's sentences. Which -ed sound do you hear in each sentence?

DESCRIBING A SOLUTION

8 Put the words and phrases in order to make statements.

1 a metro line / build / They / had to / .

_____

2 could / cycle / People / for free / .

_____

3 The cities / car sharing / started / for workers / .

_____

4 There is / moving / a / walkway / .

_____

5 is / paper tickets / faster / The Oyster card / than / .

_____

6 can tap / to pay / People / credit cards / .

_____

DESCRIBING RESULTS

9 Look at the problems, solutions and results in the table. Match the correct problems, solutions and results. Then write them in the space provided.

problem	solution	result
There was no public transport, so people had to drive everywhere.	One solution is self-driving cars.	So, these cars are safer because there are fewer accidents.
There are a lot of bad drivers, so there are a lot of accidents.	So Transport for London started Oyster cards.	That way, there were fewer cars and workers felt better.
It took a long time because people waited to buy tickets and go through the gate.	One solution was car sharing.	The result is that it is very fast and easy.

1 _____

_____

2 _____

_____

3 _____

_____

10 Work with a partner. Take turns to describe the results in Exercise 9.
Use the phrases to help you.

I think it was
a good solution.

I don't think it was
a good solution.

Why? Because …

That means …

SPEAKING TASK

Describe a transport problem, solutions and results.

PREPARE

1 Look back at the table in the Critical thinking section in Exercise 3. Review
your notes and add any new information you want to include in your
presentation.

2 Organize your talk by:

- introducing the topic.
- talking about the problem.
- talking about ideas for solutions.
- talking about what happened (the results).

3 Read the Task checklist as you prepare your talk.

TASK CHECKLIST	✔
Describe the topic.	
Describe the problem.	
Describe the solutions.	
Describe the results.	
Use *because* and *so* in the solutions and results.	
Use irregular past simple verbs correctly.	
Use correct pronunciation for regular past simple verbs with /t/, /d/ and /ɪd/.	

PRESENT

4 Work with a partner from your Critical thinking group. Take turns practising your talk. Use your notes and the photo of the city to help you.

5 Work with a partner from the other group. Take turns to describe the solution to the transport problem in Melbourne or Mexico City. Ask follow-up questions to check your understanding.

DISCUSS

6 Discuss the questions in class.

1 Which city had the best solution?
2 Is that solution a good idea for your city / country? Why / Why not?
3 Can you think of any other good solutions?

OBJECTIVES REVIEW

1 Check your learning objectives for this unit. Write *3, 2* or *1* for each objective.

3 = very well   2 = well   1 = not so well

I can ...

watch and understand a video about travelling by road.   _____

listen for definitions.   _____

synthesize information.   _____

use the past simple.   _____

use *because* and *so*.   _____

describe a topic.   _____

describe a problem.   _____

describe a solution.   _____

describe results.   _____

describe a transport problem, solution and results.   _____

2 Go to the *Unlock* Online Workbook for more practice with this unit's learning objectives.

WORDLIST		
accident (n) ⊙	metro (n)	taxi (n)
bus (n)	motorbike (n)	ticket (n)
car (n) ⊙	passenger (n)	traffic (n) ⊙
ferry (n)	pavement (n)	train (n) ⊙
idea (n) ⊙	petrol (n)	travel (v) ⊙
journey (n) ⊙	problem (n) ⊙	

⊙ = high-frequency words in the Cambridge Academic Corpus

PAIRWORK EXERCISES

STUDENT A

UNIT 1, page 27
DISCUSSION, EXERCISE 8

Think about Listening 1 and Listening 2. Ask Student B these questions about the person in photo d on page 25.

What's her name?
Where's she from?
Why is she famous?
Who are her parents?

Read this information. Then answer Student B's questions about the person in photo c on page 25.

> **Name:** Larry Page
> **Country:** the United States
> **Job:** engineer, computer scientist, businessman
> **Famous for:** started Google with a friend
> **Parents:** father, Carl Page, computer scientist / mother, Gloria Page, computer scientist

UNIT 1, page 30
PREPARATION FOR SPEAKING, EXERCISE 1

Spell the words for your partner.

1 E–G–Y–P–T–I–A–N
2 E–M–I–R–A–T–I
3 J–A–P–A–N–E–S–E

UNIT 4, page 98
SPEAKING TASK, EXERCISE 3
Group A (Student A)

Work with other students from Group A and practise giving directions from the fountain to places 1–5 on the map of The University of Alpha. Take notes.

1 the bank
2 the Language Centre
3 the Physics building
4 the History building
5 the supermarket

UNIT 4, page 100
DISCUSS, EXERCISE 5

The University of Alpha

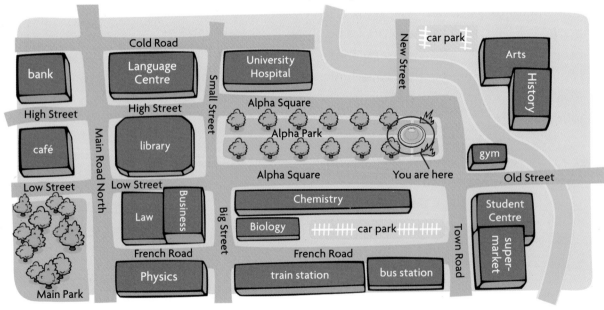

UNIT 5, page 117
LISTENING 2, EXERCISE 4

About you

My name's Alan Green and I'm from Portland, Oregon, in the US. I'm a student here at the University of Yukon. I would like to work at the sports centre after I graduate.

I'm strong, fit and I love sport. I can speak English and French. My favourite sports are football and basketball. I can also teach karate and judo.

UNIT 8, page 185
CRITICAL THINKING, EXERCISE 2
Group A

1 What is the topic?
2 What was the problem?
3 What was the solution?
4 Was it a good solution? (What was the result?)

Traffic problems and solutions for Mexico City, Santa Fe District

Mexico City is one of the biggest cities in the world. In the city's Santa Fe district, there are 850,000 journeys each day. Sixty-four percent of the journeys are for business reasons. There are no trains or high-speed buses and there isn't a metro system, so people have to drive or take old, crowded, unsafe buses everywhere. All these cars cause several problems. First, there is a lot of pollution. Forty-nine percent of the pollution comes from cars. The cars also cause problems for businesses. They need to spend a lot of money to have a car park. The traffic is bad for workers, too. It takes a long time to drive to work, so they feel tired at work. They spend more time driving to work and more money on petrol than people in places with good public transport. One solution is sharing transport with others. For example, workers use car sharing or bicycle-sharing. This way, there are fewer cars and workers feel better.

STUDENT B
UNIT 1, page 27
DISCUSSION, EXERCISE 8

Read this information. Then answer Student A's questions about the person in photo d on page 25.

> **Name:** Ursula Burns
> **Country:** the United States
> **Job:** businesswoman
> **Famous for:** first African-American female CEO of a large company in the US
> **Parent:** mother – Olga Burns, child-care centre owner

Think about Listening 1 and Listening 2. Ask Student A these questions about the person in photo c on page 25.

What's his name?
Where's he from?
Why is he famous?
Who are his parents?

UNIT 4, page 99
DISCUSS, EXERCISE 4

UNIT 1, page 30
PREPARATION FOR SPEAKING, EXERCISE 1

Spell the words for your partner.

4 T–U–R–K–I–S–H
5 A–M–E–R–I–C–A–N
6 O–M–A–N–I

UNIT 4, page 98
SPEAKING TASK, EXERCISE 3
Group B (Student B)

Work with other students from Group B and practise giving directions from the statue to places 1–5 on the map of The University of Beta. Take notes.

1 the History building
2 the train station
3 the Physics building
4 the bus station
5 the gym

The University of Beta

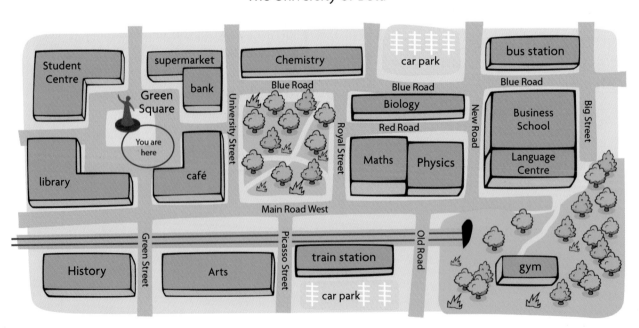

UNIT 5, page 117
LISTENING 2, EXERCISE 4

About you

I'm Lucy Lau and I'm from Vancouver, Canada. I speak English, French and Cantonese. I have a degree in Sports Science. In Vancouver, I teach zumba, pilates and yoga. I'm also a good tennis player. I think it is important to be kind and polite. A fitness instructor should help people. I would like to work with you.

UNIT 8, page 185
CRITICAL THINKING, EXERCISE 2
Group B

1 What is the topic?
2 What was the problem?
3 What was the solution?
4 Was it a good solution?
   (What was the result?)

Solution to traffic problems in Melbourne, Australia

Melbourne is a big city with a lot of people and big traffic problems. People spend many hours sitting in traffic. All of this sitting is not good for people's health. There is public transport, but many people still like to drive because the public transport isn't very good. People often have to wait 30–60 minutes for a bus. One solution to Melbourne's traffic problems is self-driving cars. Because of computer navigation in self-driving cars, they cause less traffic. And in self-driving cars, people can just sit and enjoy the ride. These cars are safer because not everyone is a good driver! So self-driving cars can stop accidents from happening. Workers can relax more and worry less when they drive, so it's good for their health and work.

GLOSSARY

⊙ = high-frequency words in the Cambridge Academic Corpus

Vocabulary	Pronunciation	Part of speech	Definition
UNIT 1			
brother ⊙	/ˈbrʌðə/	(n)	a boy or man who has the same parents as you
businessman	/ˈbɪznɪsmən/	(n)	a man who works in business, usually having an important job
businesswoman	/ˈbɪznɪswʊmən/	(n)	a woman who works in business, usually having an important job
chef	/ʃef/	(n)	someone who cooks food in a restaurant
creative ⊙	/kriˈeɪtɪv/	(adj)	good at thinking of new ideas or using imagination
doctor ⊙	/ˈdɒktə/	(n)	a person whose job is to treat people who are ill or hurt
engineer ⊙	/endʒɪˈnɪə/	(n)	someone whose job is to design, build, or repair machines, roads, bridges, etc.
family ⊙	/ˈfæməli/	(n)	a group of people who are related to each other, especially parents and children
father ⊙	/ˈfɑːðə/	(n)	someone's male parent
free ⊙	/friː/	(adj)	not costing any money
manager ⊙	/ˈmænɪdʒə/	(n)	someone in control of an office, shop, team, etc.
mother ⊙	/ˈmʌðə/	(n)	someone's female parent
scientist ⊙	/ˈsaɪəntɪst/	(n)	someone who studies science or works in science
sister ⊙	/ˈsɪstə/	(n)	a girl or woman who has the same parents as you
student ⊙	/ˈstjuːdənt/	(n)	someone who is studying at a school or university
teacher ⊙	/ˈtiːtʃə/	(n)	someone whose job is to teach in a school, college, etc.
writer ⊙	/ˈraɪtə/	(n)	someone whose job is writing books, stories, articles, etc.

Vocabulary	Pronunciation	Part of speech	Definition
UNIT 2			
autumn 🔊	/ˈɔːtəm/	(n)	the season of the year between summer and winter
black 🔊	/blæk/	(adj)	being the colour of the sky on a dark night
blue 🔊	/bluː/	(adj)	being the colour of the sky when there are no clouds
climate 🔊	/ˈklaɪmət/	(n)	the weather of a particular place
cloud 🔊	/klaʊd/	(n)	one of the white or grey things in the sky which are made of small water drops
cloudy	/ˈklaʊdi/	(adj)	with many clouds in the sky
cold 🔊	/kəʊld/	(adj)	having a low temperature
desert 🔊	/ˈdezət/	(n)	a large, hot, dry area with very few plants
equator	/ɪˈkweɪtə/	(n)	an imaginary line around the centre of the Earth
forest 🔊	/ˈfɒrɪst/	(n)	a large area of trees growing closely together
green 🔊	/griːn/	(adj)	being the colour of grass
hot 🔊	/hɒt/	(adj)	having a high temperature
inch	/ɪnʃ/	(n)	a unit of measure, about 2.5 centimetres
island 🔊	/ˈaɪlənd/	(n)	an area of land which has water around it
mountain 🔊	/ˈmaʊntɪn/	(n)	a very high hill
orange	/ˈɒrɪndʒ/	(adj)	being a colour which is a mixture of red and yellow
park 🔊	/pɑːk/	(n)	a large area of grass and trees, usually very beautiful and everybody can use it
rain 🔊	/reɪn/	(n)	water that falls from the sky in small drops
rainy	/ˈreɪni/	(adj)	raining a lot
red 🔊	/red/	(adj)	being the same colour as blood
sea 🔊	/siː/	(n)	a large area of salt water
sky	/skaɪ/	(n)	the area above the Earth where you can see clouds and the sun
snow	/snəʊ/	(n)	soft, white pieces of frozen water which fall from the sky
snowy	/ˈsnəʊi/	(adj)	snowing or covered with snow
spin	/spɪn/	(v)	to turn round and round
spring 🔊	/sprɪŋ/	(n)	the season of the year between winter and summer

Vocabulary	Pronunciation	Part of speech	Definition
storm	/stɔːm/	(n)	very bad weather with a lot of rain or snow and strong wind
stormy	/ˈstɔːmi/	(adj)	bad weather with a lot of wind and rain
summer ⊙	/ˈsʌmə/	(n)	the warmest season of the year, between spring and autumn
sun ⊙	/sʌn/	(n)	the light and heat which comes from the sun
sunny	/ˈsʌni/	(adj)	bright because of light from the sun
temperature ⊙	/ˈtemprətʃə/	(n)	how hot or cold something is
the dry season	/ðə draɪ ˈsiːzən/	(phr)	the time of year without rain
the rainy season	/ðə ˈreɪni ˈsiːzən/	(phr)	the time of year with a lot of rain
weather ⊙	/ˈweðə/	(n)	the temperature or conditions outside, for example, if it is hot, cold, sunny, etc.
white ⊙	/waɪt/	(adj)	being the colour of snow or milk
wind ⊙	/wɪnd/	(n)	a natural, fast movement of air
windy	/ˈwɪndi/	(adj)	with a lot of wind
winter ⊙	/ˈwɪntə/	(n)	the coldest season of the year, between autumn and spring
yellow ⊙	/ˈjeləʊ/	(adj)	being the same colour as a lemon or the sun

UNIT 3

Vocabulary	Pronunciation	Part of speech	Definition
busy ⊙	/ˈbɪzi/	(adj)	if you are busy, you are doing a lot
café	/ˈkæfeɪ/	(n)	a small restaurant for tea, coffee and snacks
do homework	/du ˈhəʊmwɜːk/	(v phr)	to do work which teachers give their students to do at home
exercise ⊙	/ˈeksəsaɪz/	(v)	to do an activity with your body to make your body strong
go online	/gəʊ ɒnˈlaɪn/	(v phr)	to spend time connected to the internet
go out	/gəʊ aʊt/	(v)	to spend time with friends outside your home
gym	/dʒɪm/	(n)	a place where you can go to exercise and get fit
lifestyle ⊙	/ˈlaɪfstaɪl/	(n)	the way that you live
parents ⊙	/ˈpeərənts/	(n)	your mother and father
play computer games	/pleɪ kəmˈpjuːtə ˌgeɪmz/	(v phr)	to compete or be involved in a game which is played on a computer, in which the pictures on the screen are controlled by pressing keys

Vocabulary	Pronunciation	Part of speech	Definition
sleep ⊙	/sliːp/	(v)	to be in the state of rest when your eyes are closed, your body is not active and your mind is unconscious
study ⊙	/ˈstʌdi/	(v)	to learn a particular subject, either in a school or university or by reading books
teenager	/ˈtiːnˌeɪdʒə/	(n)	someone who is between 13 and 19 years old
text ⊙	/tekst/	(v)	to send a message from one mobile phone to another
watch TV	/wɒtʃ tiːˈviː/	(v phr)	to look at television for a period of time

UNIT 4

Vocabulary	Pronunciation	Part of speech	Definition
bank ⊙	/bæŋk/	(n)	somewhere you can put your money
bridge ⊙	/brɪdʒ/	(n)	something which goes over water so people can get from one side to the other
building ⊙	/ˈbɪldɪŋ/	(n)	a house, school, hospital or office
campus	/ˈkæmpəs/	(n)	a large area for university buildings
car park	/ˈkɑː ˌpɑːk/	(n)	an area for cars
cinema	/ˈsɪnəmə/	(n)	a place where people go to watch films
department store	/dɪˈpɑːtmənt ˌstɔː/	(n)	a shop with a lot of different things, such as clothes, towels, furniture, toys, etc.
directions ⊙	/dɪˈrekʃənz/	(n)	information which tells you how to get to a place
factory ⊙	/ˈfæktəri/	(n)	a place where workers use machines to make things
food court	/ˈfuːd ˌkɔːt/	(n)	a place with many small restaurants, usually in a shopping centre
fountain	/ˈfaʊntɪn/	(n)	a beautiful tower with water coming out of it
grow ⊙	/grəʊ/	(v)	to become larger; to increase in size or amount
hospital ⊙	/ˈhɒspɪtəl/	(n)	a place to get help if you are sick or hurt
library ⊙	/ˈlaɪbrəri/	(n)	a place where people can come to study and which has a lot of books for people to take home
location ⊙	/ləʊˈkeɪʃən/	(n)	where something is
map ⊙	/mæp/	(n)	a picture which shows where countries, towns, roads, rivers, etc. are
monument ⊙	/ˈmɒnjəmənt/	(n)	something large which people visit to remember an important person or event

Vocabulary	Pronunciation	Part of speech	Definition
museum ⊙	/mjuːˈziːəm/	(n)	a place with paintings, statues and important things from history
park ⊙	/pɑːk/	(n)	a place where you can go for a walk and see a lot of trees and grass
playground	/ˈpleɪɡraʊnd/	(n)	a place with special equipment for children to play on
record ⊙	/ˈrekɔːd/	(n)	information about or a description of an event, usually on paper or in pictures
safe ⊙	/seɪf/	(adj)	not dangerous
shopping centre	/ˈʃɒpɪŋ ˌsentə/	(n)	a building with many different kinds of shops inside
skyline	/ˈskaɪ.laɪn/	(n)	the outline of buildings, mountains, etc. against the sky
supermarket	/ˈsuːpəˌmɑːkɪt/	(n)	a large shop with food to buy
toilets	/ˈtɔɪləts/	(n)	rooms in a public building where there are toilets
tower ⊙	/taʊə/	(n)	a tall, thin building or structure, for example, the Eiffel Tower in Paris, France, and the CN Tower in Toronto, Canada
train station	/ˈtreɪn ˌsteɪʃən/	(n)	somewhere you can get on a train
university ⊙	/ˌjuːnɪˈvɜːsəti/	(n)	a place where students study at a high level after secondary school
urban ⊙	/ˈɜːbən/	(adj)	of or in a city

UNIT 5

advice ⊙	/ədˈvaɪs/	(n)	suggestions about what you think someone should do
boring	/ˈbɔːrɪŋ/	(adj)	not interesting or exciting
earn	/ɜːn/	(v)	to get money for doing work
example ⊙	/ɪɡˈzɑːmpl/	(n)	something which is typical of what you are talking about
fit ⊙	/fɪt/	(adj)	healthy and strong, especially from exercising
hard ⊙	/hɑːd/	(adj)	difficult to do
help ⊙	/help/	(v)	to make it easier for someone to do something
job ⊙	/dʒɒb/	(n)	the work a person does to get money
kind ⊙	/kaɪnd/	(adj)	wanting to help others and show you care about them

Vocabulary	Pronunciation	Part of speech	Definition
polite	/pə'laɪt/	(adj)	behaving in a way which shows good manners and respect for others
strong ⊙	/strɒŋ/	(adj)	physically powerful
teach ⊙	/tiːtʃ/	(v)	to give lessons at a school or university
work ⊙	/wɜːk/	(v)	to do a job, especially a job you do to get money

UNIT 6

Vocabulary	Pronunciation	Part of speech	Definition
armchair	/'ɑːmˌtʃeə/	(n)	a comfortable chair with sides which support your arms
bookcase	/'bʊkkeɪs/	(n)	a piece of furniture with shelves for putting books on
ceiling	/'siːlɪŋ/	(n)	the top of a room which you can see when you look up
chair ⊙	/tʃeə/	(n)	a seat for one person, with a back, usually four legs, and sometimes two arms
cheap ⊙	/tʃiːp/	(adj)	not costing a lot of money
comfortable ⊙	/'kʌmftəbl/	(adj)	comfortable furniture and clothes make you feel relaxed
desk	/desk/	(n)	a table that you sit at to write or work, often with drawers
expensive ⊙	/ɪk'spensɪv/	(adj)	costing a lot of money
far ⊙	/fɑː/	(adv)	not close in location
floor ⊙	/flɔː/	(n)	what you walk on inside a building
furniture	/'fɜːnɪtʃə/	(n)	things such as chairs, tables and beds which you put in a home or office
glass ⊙	/glɑːs/	(adj, n)	a hard, see-through material, used to make windows, bottles, etc.
lamp	/læmp/	(n)	a piece of equipment which produces light
leather	/'leðə/	(adj, n)	the skin of animals used to make things such as shoes and bags
metal ⊙	/'metəl/	(adj, n)	a hard, shiny material used to make knives and forks, bicycles and machines
modern ⊙	/'mɒdən/	(adj)	using the newest ideas, design, technology, etc.
near ⊙	/nɪə/	(adv, prep)	very close in location
noisy	/'nɔɪzi/	(adj)	making a lot of noise
plastic ⊙	/'plæstɪk/	(adj, n)	a material which can be made into different shapes, e.g. water bottles

Vocabulary	Pronunciation	Part of speech	Definition
quiet ⊙	/kwaɪət/	(adj)	making little noise or no noise
room ⊙	/ruːm/	(n)	what the inside of a building is made up of
sofa	/ˈsəʊfə/	(n)	a large, comfortable seat for more than one person
table ⊙	/ˈteɪbl/	(n)	a piece of furniture with four legs, used for eating off, putting things on, etc.
uncomfortable	/ʌnˈkʌmftəbl/	(adj)	not feeling comfortable and pleasant
wall ⊙	/wɔːl/	(n)	one of the sides of a room
wood ⊙	/wʊd/	(n)	the hard material which trees are made of
wooden	/ˈwʊdən/	(adj)	made of wood

UNIT 7

Vocabulary	Pronunciation	Part of speech	Definition
burger	/ˈbɜːgə/	(n)	meat which is pressed into a circle and fried
chips	/tʃɪps/	(n)	long thin pieces of potato which are fried
culture ⊙	/ˈkʌltʃə/	(n)	the usual way of living in a country or for a group of people
dish	/dɪʃ/	(n)	food which is prepared in a special way and given a name
enjoy ⊙	/ɪnˈdʒɔɪ/	(v)	to get pleasure from something
fast food	/ˌfɑːst ˈfuːd/	(n)	food which is served very quickly in a restaurant because it is already prepared
favourite ⊙	/ˈfeɪvərət/	(adj)	your favourite person or thing is the one you like best
fish ⊙	/fɪʃ/	(n)	an animal which lives in water and swims using its tail and fins
healthy ⊙	/ˈhelθi/	(adj)	good for your health
home-cooked	/ˌhəʊm ˈkʊkt/	(adj)	when food is cooked at home
international ⊙	/ˌɪntəˈnæʃənəl/	(adj)	from more than one country
meal	/miːl/	(n)	the food which you eat at breakfast, lunch or dinner
meat ⊙	/miːt/	(n)	parts of animals used as food
noodles	/ˈnuː.dəlz/	(n)	long thin strips of food, made from flour or rice with water
pasta	/ˈpæs.tə/	(n)	food made from water and flour (and egg) in different shapes, e.g. spaghetti
pizza	/ˈpiːt.sə/	(n)	a circle of flat bread with cheese and tomato sauce (and sometimes meat or vegetables)

Vocabulary	Pronunciation	Part of speech	Definition
rice ⊙	/raɪs/	(n)	small, white or brown grains from a plant which are cooked and eaten
salad	/ˈsæl.əd/	(n)	a mixture of uncooked/cooked vegetables, often with lettuce and tomatoes
sandwich	/ˈsæn.wɪdʒ/	(n)	two pieces of bread with cheese or meat between them, usually eaten cold
taco	/ˈtæk.əʊ/	(n)	a hard, folded tortilla with meat or cheese inside, often with a sauce
vegetable	/ˈvedʒtəbl/	(n)	a plant which is used as food

UNIT 8

Vocabulary	Pronunciation	Part of speech	Definition
accident ⊙	/ˈæksɪdənt/	(n)	a bad situation which is not expected and which causes pain or problems
bus	/bʌs/	(n)	a big vehicle which takes many people around a city
ferry	/ˈferi/	(n)	a boat which regularly carries passengers and vehicles across an area of water
idea ⊙	/aɪˈdɪə/	(n)	a suggestion or plan for doing something
journey ⊙	/ˈdʒɜːni/	(n)	travelling from one place to another in a car, bus, train, the metro, etc.
metro	/ˈmetrəʊ/	(n)	trains which travel underground in a city
motorbike	/ˈməʊ.tə.baɪk/	(n)	a bike with an engine
passenger	/ˈpæsəndʒə/	(n)	someone who travels in a car, bus, etc., but doesn't drive it
pavement	/ˈpeɪvmənt/	(n)	a hard path for people to walk on next to a road
petrol	/ˈpetrəl/	(n)	what most cars need in order to move
problem ⊙	/ˈprɒbləm/	(n)	something which makes life difficult and needs a solution
taxi	/ˈtæksi/	(n)	a car with a driver who you pay to take you somewhere
ticket	/ˈtɪkɪt/	(n)	a small piece of paper which shows you paid to do something
traffic ⊙	/ˈtræfɪk/	(n)	the cars, trucks, etc. driving on the road
train ⊙	/treɪn/	(n)	a long, thin type of car which travels on metal tracks and carries people or things
travel ⊙	/ˈtrævəl/	(v)	to go from one place to another, usually over a long distance

UNIT 1

▶ **A clothes maker and a furniture maker in Johannesburg**

Narrator: This is Soweto, in Johannesburg, South Africa. These colourful towers are famous buildings in Soweto. Mandisa Zwane is a businesswoman. She lives and works in Soweto. She designs and sews clothes that are made from colourful African material. Her business is growing. Four other people work in her business. She sells her clothes to shops in Europe and North America. She is proud of her work, her business and her home in Soweto.

Mandisa Zwane: ... because this is where I do my business, this is where I've hired people, and it's quite successful.

Narrator: There are many other new small businesses in Soweto. Some sell things for the home, like dishes and cushions; others sell art. All these new businesses in Soweto get help from an organization called the Box Shop. The Box Shop helps small businesses get started. It gives advice and helps owners to buy equipment for their businesses. It also helps these small businesses find buyers all over the world. Valaphi Mpolweni is another businessman who works with Box Shop. Like Mandisa, he lives and works in Soweto. He designs and makes furniture. He sells the furniture to stores in the United States. With help from Box Shop, his business is now very successful.

🔊 **1.1**

See script on page 19.

🔊 **1.2**

Carlos: Hi, hello. I'm Carlos. I'm going to tell you about Koko. She's a **student** in our class. She's 18 and she's from Japan. Her **family's** from Sapporo. Her father's a teacher. She wants to study English at university.

Kerry: A-l-l right! Thank you, Carlos. So, Koko. It's your turn. Please introduce the student next to you.

Koko: Hi! I'm going to tell you about Nehir. Nehir is 19. She's from Turkey. She has a brother. Her family has a hotel. Her **mother** and **father** are the **managers**. Nehir wants to study Business at university.

Kerry: Thank you, Koko. Nehir – your turn!

Nehir: Hello. I'm going to tell you about Carlos. He's 19. He's from Peru. His father's an **engineer** and his mother's a **doctor**. Carlos wants to study Computer Science at university.

Kerry: Thank you, Nehir.

🔊 **1.3**

A

Kerry: Who's your best friend, Yasemin?

Yasemin: Her name is Meral.

Kerry: How old is she?

Yasemin: She's 20.

Kerry: Is she from Turkey?

Yasemin: Yes, but she isn't from Ankara like me. She's from İzmir.

B

Kayo: Excuse me, Kerry. Are you from Sydney?

Kerry: No, no, I'm not from Australia. I'm from England. But my grandparents are Australian. They're not from Sydney. They're from Melbourne.

Kayo: Are your parents English?

Kerry: Yes – and my sisters. We're all English.

🔊 1.4

See script on page 26.

🔊 1.5

Marie: Hi, everybody! Good morning! My name is Marie.

All: Hi. / Morning. / Hello.

Marie: OK, so I'm going to tell you about a famous person. She's from the UK. It's photo 'a'. Who is this, in the photo?

Student 1: Is she a **businesswoman**?

Marie: No, she isn't a businesswoman.

Student 2: Um, is she a **writer**? And maybe a **chef** too?

Marie: Yes! That's it! She's a famous chef. Her name's Nadiya Hussain. She also writes cookery books. And she presents a TV show about cooking, too. She's famous for her wonderful desserts. She's very creative. She and her family are British. Her husband's name is Abdal. He's a manager at a computer company. He's also a great husband and father. She also has three children – two sons and a daughter. Their names are Musa, Dawud and Maryam.

Clare: Thanks, Marie. Hi, everyone! My name is Clare. Now, I'm going to tell you about my person. Do you know him? In photo 'b'?

Student 2: Oh he is wearing a suit. Is he a **businessman**?

Clare: Well, he *did* start his own business. He's Salman Khan. He's American. Salman's a **scientist** and a **teacher**. He's famous for his free school, the Khan Academy. All the classes are on the internet. The students are from many countries. Salman's from California in the US, but his father's from Bangladesh and his mother's from India. His wife's a doctor and they have a son and a daughter.

🔊 1.6

1 I'm going to tell you about a famous person from Mexico.

2 Ana García is a famous Mexican chef.

3 This is Haruki Murakami.

4 He's a famous Japanese writer.

🔊 1.7

See script on page 32.

🔊 1.8

See script on page 42.

UNIT 2

▶ **How deserts are formed**

This is the Sonoran Desert in North America. It's 2,000 miles north of the equator.

In the summer, the temperature can reach 122 degrees Fahrenheit. But it's not a desert because it's hot. It's a desert because there isn't much water.

Here it only rains about three inches a year, so there are very different plants and animals in a desert than in a rainforest. Where does the hot, dry air come from? It comes from near the equator.

Because the Earth spins, hot air from the equator moves high in the air, travels north, and then comes down in the Sonoran Desert. And this doesn't just happen in North America. It happens around the world.

There's the Thar Desert in India, the Arabian Desert in the Middle East, and, of course, the Sahara Desert in North Africa. Hot dry air from near the equator made all of these deserts.

That's why all of these places have hot, dry climates.

 2.1

1 Take a look at the photos.
2 They are all from one place.
3 There's a beautiful beach next to a big lake.
4 It's winter and there's a mountain.
5 It's hot and there's sand.

🔊 2.2

Teacher: OK, so today I want to talk about a place with extreme **temperatures**. Take a look at the photos. What seasons do you see?

Student 1: Summer

Teacher: Uh, huh.

Student 2: Winter

Teacher: Yes, that's right.

Student 3: **Autumn**.

Teacher: And?

Student 4: **Spring**?

Teacher: Yes, and they're all from one place – the central part of Hokkaido in Japan. It has hot summers and **cold** winters.

Let's look at photo 'a'. What can we see? Well, it's a **hot** day in summer. And there's a beautiful lake and a beach. There's a blue sky and it's sunny. There are some beautiful lakes in central Hokkaido, so people like to swim and fish.

Now here, in photo 'b', it's winter. There's lots of **snow**. It's also very cold. The temperature can get to -12 °C.

In photo 'c', you can see it's autumn. The temperature is a little cold and the trees change colour to red and orange. There are many trees in Hokkaido, so it's very beautiful.

And now we see spring in photo 'd'. After the cold **weather**, spring is welcome in Hokkaido. The weather is warm so the flowers grow.

As you can see, central Hokkaido is a place with four seasons and extreme temperatures in winter. But, it's a beautiful place, so people like to do things outside.

🔊 2.3

1 Canada gets a lot of snow in winter.
2 Summer in Washington, DC begins in June. It gets very hot.
3 Spring in London is from March to May. There are a lot of beautiful flowers.
4 In autumn, the trees change colour from green to orange or red.
5 In Korea, Japan and China, the rainy season begins in June and ends in July. It gets very wet.
6 The dry season in Brazil begins in May. There is not a lot of rain.

🔊 2.4

1 There's a river in the photo.
2 There's water in the lake.
3 There are stones on the beach.
4 There's a lot of wind in April.
5 There's a small town in the mountains.
6 There are black clouds in the sky.
7 There are extreme temperatures in the winter.
8 There's white sand on the beach.

🔊 2.5

Daniela: OK, so, good morning, everybody. I'm Daniela. OK, so, er, I'm going to talk about two photos of a place in spring. I'm from Naples in Italy and I don't like to talk about cold places or places in winter – no, really, it's true!

OK, so here's my first photo. This isn't in Italy. It's in Turkey. It's actually an **island**.

And there's a small town here. You can see there is a white building. It's a beautiful day in spring – blue **sky**, very sunny, very nice. There's a nice **forest** and it's good to go there when it's a hot day. And there's the **sea**, which is beautiful and blue.

So I chose this photo because …

Altan: Hello, everybody! OK, so, I'm Altan. I'm from Samsun. Er, Samsun is in Turkey, I'm Turkish and Samsun's a city by the Black Sea. But, OK, so today I'm going to talk about a different place.

Here's my first photo. It's a beautiful place. You can see there's a big **mountain**, and there are trees here. It's sunny, but it's a cold day in autumn. Can you see the colour of the trees? All red and orange.

So, where is this beautiful place? Well, it's in South Korea. This is Seoraksan National **Park**. It's a famous park. A lot of people go there. Here's another photo of the park …

🔊 2.6

a Good morning, everybody.
b I'm going to talk about two photos of a place in spring.
c OK, so here's my first photo.
d Hello, everybody! I'm Altan.
e I'm from Samsun. Samsun is in Turkey.
f Here's my first photo.
g Here's another photo of the park.

🔊 2.7

OK, so today I want to talk about a place with extreme temperatures. Take a look at the photos. What seasons do you see?

🔊 2.8

Khaled: Hello, everybody! OK, so I'm Khaled. I'm from Port Said in Egypt. Today I'm going to talk about two photos of a place in spring. Here's my first photo. You can see there's a big mountain. There's a lot of snow. And there are trees. The trees are orange and red. Right, so where is this place? It's in Japan. This is Mount Fuji.

Here's another photo of the mountain. There's a path and you can see there are people there. There are a lot of white clouds below. It's a beautiful place. I want to go there.

UNIT 3

▶ Festival of the Winds

Narrator: Welcome to Sydney, Australia's largest city, home to more than 5 million people.

The Opera House is Sydney's most famous building, but the city also has beautiful beaches.

This is Bondi Beach. It's only about 7 kilometres from the centre of the city. People come here to swim, surf, run, walk or just enjoy the weather. On most days, the sky above Bondi Beach is empty, but on one Sunday every year, it's filled with colourful kites.

The Festival of the Winds brings people from all over the world. They come to fly their kites. There are kites in all different shapes and sizes.

This one is a traditional diamond-shape, but there are also box kites, flag kites, fighting kites and kites in the shape of dragons, fish, sharks and even rabbits. Later in the day, these kites will fly high above the beach.

More than two thousand people come to the festival every year.

Beginners come to make their own kites or try flying a kite for the first time. Experienced people enter their kites in contests.

Which kite flies the highest? Which is the most beautiful?

It's a great way to spend time outdoors and find new friends.

At the Festival of Winds, kite lovers come to fly their kites, but most visitors come just to watch and take photos of the magnificent kites, the beautiful beaches and the clear blue skies to share with their family and friends.

🔊 3.1

See script on page 63.

🔊 3.2

See script on page 63.

🔊 3.3

Teacher: Good morning, everybody.

Students: Good morning. / Hello. / Hi.

Teacher: So, today we're going to look at lifestyles ... the lifestyles of teenagers. So, who's between the ages of 13 and 19?

Students: I am. I'm 19. / Me, too. / I'm 18.

Teacher: Then you are all teenagers. Anyone else? OK, so let's talk about **sleep**. How many hours do you sleep every night? Yes, Abdul?

Abdul: Um ... I sleep maybe six or seven hours every night.

Teacher: OK. Anyone else? Yes, Beatrice, how many hours do you sleep?

Beatrice: I don't sleep a lot. I sleep maybe five hours.

Teacher: OK. Yes, Ana, and you?

Ana: Not enough. I only sleep five or six hours a night during the week.

Teacher: You're right. That's not enough, especially for teenagers. How many hours do you think teenagers need?

Abdul: A lot!

Teacher: Yes, you're right about that. Teenagers need ten or more hours every night. So, what do you usually do at night? Are you busy? Yes, Abdul?

Abdul: At night, I like to **play computer games**.

Teacher: OK. Anyone else? Yes, Madiha.

Madiha: Well, I usually **watch TV**.

Beatrice: I **go online** or **text** friends.

Teacher: And then you **do** the **homework** for this class, of course.
So, let me ask you, what do you do on Saturday and Sunday? Yes, Sung-oh?

Sung-oh: Well, I also play computer games on Saturday and Sunday.

Teacher: Right, and what about you, Mimi?

Mimi: Um, well, I watch TV or go online.

Teacher: What else do you do? Do you **exercise**? Exercise is also very important for teenagers. It's important for all of us. Do you exercise, Sandra?

Sandra: Er, to be honest, I don't really exercise.

Teacher: Anyone else? ... Well, let's think of some things teenagers need to do to stay healthy and do well in your courses ...

🔊 3.4

See script on page 72.

🔊 3.5

April: Good morning! Can I ask you –

Woman 1: Sorry, sorry! No time! No time!

April: Excuse me! Do you have –

Woman 2: Sorry! Can't stop! That's my bus!

April: Excuse me! Can I have a few minutes of your time?

Jumana: Er, yes, sure.

April: Great! My name's April. I'm a university student and I'm asking people questions about their lifestyle. I'd like to ask you some questions – is that OK?

Jumana: Yes, no problem. I'm Jumana.

April: Great! Nice to meet you, Jumana! OK, so, um, well, I'll just start, then? OK, so do you live with your **parents**?

Jumana: Yes.

April: And do you work or **study**?

Jumana: Oh, I study – I'm a student.

April: And what do you study?

Jumana: I study Biology. I'd like to be a scientist.

April: Hmm. OK, and do you have a **busy** lifestyle?

Jumana: Yes, I think so. I have a lot of homework.

April: I see, OK, and what things do you do to relax?

Jumana: Hm. Well, I go to a **gym**. I exercise a lot.

April: Really?

Jumana: Yes. I am happy when I exercise.

April: Yes, I know what you mean. And when do you go to the gym?

Jumana: Oh, every day.

April: Every day? Wow. OK, and what other things do you do? Do you go to the cinema, for example?

Jumana: No, not really. I watch films on my computer at home.

April: I see. And what about your friends? When do you **go out** with them?

Jumana: Oh, well, I have some friends at the gym. But I also go out on Saturday afternoons. We go to a **café** and have some coffee and talk about ... well, we talk about life, people we know, that kind of thing.

April: I think I know what you mean! OK, so ...

🔊 3.6

This is Rabia. She's from Turkey. She takes the bus to the university every day. The bus comes at 7:30. Rabia arrives at 8:30. She has a Biology class at nine on Tuesday and Thursday. On Wednesday, she has lunch with her friends at 12:30. On Thursday, Rabia has an English class at three o'clock in the afternoon. She goes to the cinema with her family on Friday evening. On Saturday, she exercises in the morning. On Sunday, she does her homework in the evening. She has a busy week.

🔊 3.7

texts	studies
sleeps	watches
needs	chooses
goes	

🔊 3.8

See script on page 77.

UNIT 4

▶ **Urbanization in China**

Today, more and more people live in cities. In 1970, only two cities in the world had more than ten million people.

Now, there are more than 20, and the number is growing. These urban areas are important for our future. And there's a lot of work to keep a megacity going and growing.

Welcome to Shanghai, one of China's largest cities. Its skyline – the view of its buildings against the sky – has changed a lot over the past 20 years.

One man has an interesting record of the changes in his hometown. Two times every year, Yao Jin Yang goes to the top of the Oriental Pearl Tower and he takes pictures of the Shanghai skyline.

Mr Yao started taking pictures in 1993. Then, this tower was the tallest building in Shanghai and had the best view of the city. Today the city looks very different. His photos show how fast people can change their world.

In China, lots of people started moving from the country to the city more than 30 years ago. Now, 10,000 people move to Shanghai every week.

This kind of change is happening all over China and in many parts of the world.

🔊 4.1

1 Where is this photo from?
2 ... there's a shop here and a library there.
3 Yes, that's a bank over there.
4 The library is here.

🔊 4.2

Salesperson: Welcome, everyone. Thank you for coming to our presentation for our new app, Familynet.

Families are very busy today. Every day parents go to work and, well, children need to go everywhere. They go to school. They go to the park. They play sports or go to a friend's house. Often, teenagers can go to places by themselves. But parents want to be sure they are **safe**. With the Familynet app, they are. Parents can find the **location** of their children anywhere, anytime. And children can find the location of their parents anywhere, anytime. Do you know where your children are right now? Do you know which street or **building**? Do you have **directions** to find them? I do with this app. And I have two teenagers and an eight-year-old.

Let me show you how it works.

Look at the screenshot, please. There's a **map**. You can see the location of three children. This is the location of my three children right now. This is my son. He's at the park. That's my daughter. She's opposite the **library**. And there's her little sister. She's by the school bus. The app will tell me when she's close to home. That's nice, because I can come out when she arrives. My children are safe. I can see their location.

For my teenagers, they can go to places without their mum and dad. This makes them happy. And it makes their parents happy. You may think your teenagers will not like the app. My teenagers are no different. But, now they can go to places when we can't take them. So, they like the app now. Our app is easy to use. Just download it to your phone and open it! Try it now to find everyone in your family.

🔊 4.3

1
A: Where's the library? Is it near here?
B: Yes, it's behind the river.
2
A: Is there a bank near here?
B: Yes. There's one over the bridge. Can you see it?
3
A: Where's the famous monument?
B: It's between the university and the river.
4
A: Excuse me. Where's the factory?
B: It's by the river.
5
A: I can't find the museum. Is it near here?
B: No. It's there on the left. It's next to the park.
6
A: Where's the university?
B: It's opposite those houses.
7
A: Where can I find the train station?
B: It's behind a tall building.
8
A: I'm looking for the fountain. Is it in the park?
B: Yes. It's there in the park.

4.4

Teacher: OK, class. You now know your way around **campus**, but I know some of you like to go shopping. And it's very easy to get lost in a big **shopping centre**. So, today, let's practise what to say if you are lost. Everybody, look at the map, please. I'll begin. Ana, can you tell me where **car park** 1 is?

Ana: Yes, it's on West Street, opposite entrance 1.

Teacher: Good, Ana. Hassan, I'm at the **department store**. How do I get to the **cinema**?

Hassan: Go out of the shop and go left on path A. When you get to path B, turn left again. The cinema is on your right.

Teacher: Well done, Hassan! Altan, I'm on North Street. Can you tell me how to get to the **supermarket**?

Altan: Yes, go east. Then, turn right on East Street and follow it until you see the supermarket. It's on your right, next to the bus station.

Teacher: Excellent, Altan! OK, now I'm lost. I'm in this shoe shop. Excuse me, miss. Where are the **toilets**?

Luisa: Oh, that's easy. They're opposite you next to the stairs.

Teacher: Well done, Luisa. OK, Kana. I'm at the cinema. Can you tell me how to find the **playground**?

Kana: Er … yes. Go along path B and go through the **food court**. It's behind the food court and the shoe shop.

Teacher: OK, Kana! Now, I'm looking for the computer shop. I'm at the food court. Where can I find it?

Ana: Just go south on path A. It's on your right between the department store and the lift.

Teacher: Very good, Ana. Thank you. Now, everyone, work with a partner and practise asking for and giving directions for the next map which, is a **hospital** – I don't want you to get lost!

4.5

1 It's opposite the Business school.
2 It's in Green Square.
3 Go through Alpha Park to the Student Centre.
4 It's in front of that big fountain. There – on the right.
5 OK, then, so we're at the Language school.
6 Go along French Road.
7 There's one next to the train station.
8 It's there on the left. It's behind that school.

4.6

1 Where's the supermarket?
2 Is the Physics building near here?
3 How do I get to the Language Centre?
4 Can you tell me how to get to the History building?
5 I'm looking for the Maths building. Is it near here?

4.7

See script on page 96.

4.8

1 Excuse me! Can you tell me how to get to the History building, please?
2 Excuse me! I think I'm lost. Is the Physics building near here?
3 Excuse me! How do I get to the Language Centre?

🔊 4.9

See script on page 97.

UNIT 5

▶ Burj Khalifa

This is the Burj Khalifa in Dubai in the United Arab Emirates. It's the world's tallest building. It's more than half a mile, or over 800 metres, tall.

The Burj Khalifa is taller than any other building in the world, but it has one problem – its windows still get dirty.

These are the men who clean the world's highest windows. They work thousands of feet above the ground every day.

Johnny Salvador is the manager of a team of 15 people who clean the Burj's 24,000 windows.

When they are working, the men have to be very careful. It's very windy, and the winds are the strongest at the top.

Johnny's team must work for three months to clean all of the windows of the Burj Khalifa. It's a dangerous but exciting job.

🔊 5.1

See script on page 108.

🔊 5.2

1 I have to choose a course.
2 I have two questions to ask you.
3 You have to work hard.
4 He has to study at university.
5 He has two options: Maths or Biology.
6 She has to decide what to do.
7 You have to do four subjects.

🔊 5.3

Adviser: Come in!

Beatrice: Hello! It's, er, I'm Beatrice.

Adviser: Ah, yes, Beatrice! Please, come in. Take a seat.

Beatrice: Thank you.

Adviser: So, how can I help you?

Beatrice: Well, I want to go to university next year.

Adviser: Uh-huh.

Beatrice: I have to choose a subject to study ... but I don't know what to do. I need your **advice**. Should I go to Medical school, or should I go to music college? Should I be a doctor? A musician? I'm not sure what the best option is.

Adviser: Hmm. Those are good questions. Tell me about music school.

Beatrice: Well, there aren't many **jobs** for musicians. Well, OK, I'm sorry. That's not true. There are a lot of jobs in music – but it's a **hard** life. They **work** hard, but many musicians don't **earn** a lot of money.

Adviser: I see. And what about Medical school?

Beatrice: Er, a doctor's life ... It's a good job. It's not **boring**, and you can earn good money and **help** people.

Adviser: Yes, that's true.

Beatrice: But ... I don't know. Medical school's difficult. You have to work hard.

Adviser: Hmm. What do your parents say?

Beatrice: Well, my mother thinks I should go to Medical school.

Adviser: Why?

Beatrice: Oh, because my grades are good. I have good grades in Science and English.

Adviser: And what about your father?

Beatrice: He says I can be a doctor or an engineer or, well, anything I guess. What do you think? What should I do?

Adviser: Well, you're a good student, and you have good grades. But for now, I think you should get a job.

Beatrice: What? Why?

Adviser: Listen, I don't think you should go to university now because you don't know if you want to be a musician or a doctor ... or an engineer! I think you should get a job. Then you can go to university later when you know what ...

🔊 5.4

1 Fatima has two jobs.
2 Mark has to work very hard.
3 I have a very good job.
4 Engineers have a difficult job.
5 Paul has an important job.
6 Builders have to work fast.

🔊 5.5

See script on page 113.

🔊 5.6

Paul: Morning, Emma! And how are you today?

Emma: I'm fine thanks, Paul.

Paul: Good, good. Now then – what do you have for me here?

Emma: Well, here are two people for the job at the sports centre.

Paul: I see. Which job is this? Is it for the fitness instructor? Or for the sports-centre nurse?

Emma: This is for the fitness instructor. We're going to look at people for the nurse's job next week.

Paul: Ah, next week. OK, I see. So, who's this?

Emma: Well, this is Alan Green.

Paul: Ah, I see he's an American.

Emma: Yes. What do you think?

Paul: Well, he's **strong** and **fit** ... and he does a lot of sports: football, basketball, karate, judo. That's great.

Emma: But ... ?

Paul: But he's a student. I think a good fitness instructor should be a good teacher. I want a person who has experience – a person who can **teach** me tennis or volleyball.

Emma: OK, well, here's Lucy Lau.

Paul: Hmm. Ah, good! She's a sports scientist ... and she's a fitness instructor! That's great! So, I think Lucy is our new fitness instructor. What do you think?

Emma: Well ...

Paul: You're not sure?

Emma: Lucy is very good. But I think a fitness instructor has to be strong and fit. I think he – or she – has to be a good **example** for the students.

Paul: Interesting, go on.

Emma: We want a person who can make the students work hard. Lucy says, 'It is important to be **kind** and **polite**.' That's a good idea. But if you want to get fit, you have to work hard. I think Alan can help people do that.

Paul: I see, I see. But I think we should choose Lucy. She teaches zumba, pilates and yoga – and these are very popular right now.

Emma: Mm, that's true. Would you like me to write to Lucy and tell her the good news?

Paul: Yes, I think that would be …

🔊 5.7

See script on page 122.

🔊 5.8

1 Nurses have to work hard.
2 The sports centre nurse has to speak another language.
3 Morena and Darren have experience in a hospital.
4 Morena has a job in a small hospital.

UNIT 6

▶ **Monticello and Jefferson**

This beautiful building is Monticello, in Virginia. It's the home of Thomas Jefferson, the third President of the United States, from 1797 to 1801. He is very important to Americans because he wrote the Declaration of Independence.

He lived in this house in Virginia, United States. The house has thirty-three rooms. And it's an important, interesting part of American history.

It took more than forty years for Jefferson to finish building Monticello, in 1809. He wanted to build a home that looked different for his new country. So he combined Italian, English and French styles.

When you go through the front door, you enter the Indian Hall. On the walls, there are many Native American and hunting items from the new world.

But in other rooms, like this one, the styles are from European cultures.

Also on the first floor is Jefferson's private area, including his bedroom and study. He wanted his house to be convenient and comfortable.

When he got out of bed in the morning, he could go directly into his study and start working – on Science, farming or Politics.

Monticello also had 5,000 acres of land, with many gardens and a large working farm.

Today it is a living museum – a memory of early American history.

🔊 6.1

See script on page 131.

🔊 6.2

Paul: Good evening. I'm Paul Clark, and welcome to *Think Design*. I have a special guest today – Dr Kay Thompson. Dr Thompson is a psychologist and an author of many books. Welcome, Dr Thompson. Now, you're not an architect, but you help design buildings. What do you do?

Dr Thompson: Well, I help architects choose good colours for their buildings.

Paul: Is colour important?

Dr Thompson: Yes. Very important. Why? Because colour can change the way we think, the way we feel, even the way we talk.

Paul: Really?

Dr Thompson: Yes. For example, many restaurants in Mexico have orange **walls**.

Paul: Why?

Dr Thompson: Well, what do you think?

Paul: Oh, um, I don't know, er, is orange a warm colour? Is it a friendly colour?

Dr Thompson: Those are good ideas. But, no. The walls are orange because some experts think that orange makes people feel hungry.

Paul: Hungry? How interesting! But ... is that true? You don't see many orange restaurants in London, for example. Why is that?

Dr Thompson: Because colours mean different things in different countries. For example, if you go on the internet and look for photographs of 'Chinese restaurants', you're going to see a lot of red! Red walls, red **floors**, maybe even red **ceilings**!

Paul: Why? Do they think that red makes people feel hungry?

Dr Thompson: Good question, but no. Many Chinese restaurants are red because in China red is the colour of fire, of happiness and of all the good things in life.

Paul: I see. This is really interesting. So what about the UK? If my friend opens a restaurant, what colour should it be?

Dr Thompson: Well, if you mean traditional British food, white is a good colour – white and also a **wood** colour in a **room**.

Paul: Oh? Why?

Dr Thompson: Because natural things are important to many people in the UK. White means fresh and clean, and the wood colours – brown, yellow – are natural. And nature is healthy.

Paul: I see, so **furniture** must be important, too. If the tables and chairs are traditional or modern, for example.

Dr Thompson: Well, that's another ...

🔊 **6.3**

armchair, table, chair, bookcase, lamp, desk, sofa

🔊 **6.4**

comfortable, glass, leather, metal, plastic, uncomfortable, wooden

🔊 **6.5**

Dale: ... thanks for the coffee, Hakan! Very nice!

Hakan: Yes, it's good Turkish coffee. OK, then. Should we start?

Dale: Yes, I think so. OK, so we need a place for our new office. What about here?

Hakan: Where?

Dale: The city centre. What do you think?

Hakan: Well, it's a good place. It's **near** some good roads. But ... I don't think we should go there.

Dale: Oh? Why not?

Hakan: Because the buildings in the centre are very old. They are cold in winter and hot in summer, and they're very **noisy**. They're uncomfortable places.

Dale: Oh, I see. That's not good.

Hakan: No. And the buildings there are **expensive**.

Dale: Really?

Hakan: Yes. My sister's a lawyer and her office is in the centre. She likes her job, but she doesn't like her building.

Dale: OK, so not there, then! Hmm. What about here?

Hakan: The park?

Dale: Yes. It's **quiet**, and it's not **far** from a big road. What do you think?

Hakan: Hmm, I'm not sure. It's pretty far from the centre. What about here? Near the train station?

Dale: The train station is good. It's good for travel ... but I think we should go to the park. The buildings near the train station aren't **cheap**.

Hakan: They're not?

Dale: No. They're really expensive.

Hakan: OK, let's go with the park. I'm happy with that. Now, what about the design? I think we should have a **modern** design with big windows. What about you?

Dale: Yes, I agree. Big windows are good. What about the walls? What colour do you think we should paint the walls?

Hakan: Hmm. What about blue?

Dale: Blue's a good colour, but I'm not sure. Blue can make people feel cold.

Hakan: Ah, yes, that's true. What about yellow? Because it's a warm and sunny colour.

Dale: Yes, you're right. Yellow's a good colour. OK, so what's next? Ah, OK, furniture. So what do you think?

Hakan: Well, I think we should have modern desks and chairs. The desks can be made of metal and wood. Then, we can have comfortable chairs. It will all be new and beautiful.

🔊 6.6

See script on page 142.

UNIT 7

▶ The price of perfect fruit

Narrator: A good gift for someone special in Japan is a piece of luxury fruit. Perhaps your boss or your husband's parents. It's not ordinary fruit. You can buy it only in special shops.

Luxury fruit is very expensive because it is so beautiful. Each piece of fruit is perfect – the perfect size, shape and colour. But it also smells and tastes wonderful.

The manager of this luxury fruit shop explains why it is so expensive. Each piece of fruit gets a lot of care and attention. This melon costs 175 US dollars.

This peach? $30. The grapes? $95.

This woman is buying a special dessert for her family. A cup of fruit costs $30. She says it's like eating a cake. It makes you feel happy.

Most people don't buy luxury fruit for themselves. They give it as a gift. When you give luxury fruit, this shows that you think the person is very important. These young women love gifts of luxury fruit.

Melons like these are the most expensive of all. The price for these two perfect melons was $16,000 – about the same price as a car!

🔊 7.1

See script on page 153.

🔊 7.2

1

Speaker A: Is the number of people there about seventy million?

Speaker B: Er, no, I think it's about seventeen.

Speaker A: Seventeen million? OK, thanks.

2

Speaker A: We feed sixty children from poor families here.

Speaker B: Sorry – how many children? Sixteen?

Speaker A: No, sixty.

3

Speaker A: Thirteen percent of this class are vegetarians – people who don't eat meat.

Speaker B: Thirty? Are you sure?

Speaker A: No, no – thirteen!

4

Speaker A: People in this city eat fifteen thousand tonnes of beef every month.

Speaker B: Is that true? Fifty thousand tonnes every month?

Speaker A: No, fifteen thousand – not fifty.

🔊 7.3

Teacher: OK, everyone. So today I'd like to talk about traditions and food in the past and present. For example, in the past, **meat** was expensive or was not available. My grandparents only had meat on special holidays. But now, in the UK, meat is always available. The average person in the UK eats meat once a day. That's quite often! What do you think? Are meat **dishes** as special now? How about in your family? Yes, Yuki?

Yuki: Well, my grandparents ate a lot of **fish**.

Teacher: Uh-huh, where did they live?

Yuki: In Japan. They lived by the water, so it was easy to get. Everyone ate fish and **rice** and **vegetables**. People made our traditional dishes with that.

Teacher: Do they still do this today?

Yuki: Yeah, but today we have foods from everywhere. Italian food is very popular in Japan now.

José: This is the same in my country, Mexico. Fifty years ago, my grandmother cooked traditional dishes at home every day. But now, there are so many **international** foods available in the supermarket, like Middle Eastern, Chinese or Italian. They're cheap and already prepared, so there's no need to make them at home.

Teacher: So, everyone, do you think these international dishes are like the dishes your grandmother made?

Yuki / José / Others: No. / No way. / Uh-uh.

Teacher: In fact, José, do you know how to cook?

José: No, I never learned. We moved a lot. My parents both worked, so they didn't cook very much. We ate a lot of **fast food**. You know, burgers and chips. It wasn't very healthy, I know.

Teacher: OK, so let me take a quick survey. How many of you know how to cook? ... Uh ... 13, no, only 14 students out of 30?! Well, can any of you cook traditional dishes? Hmm ... only 20%! I guess this isn't a surprise. So, what do you think? Now that we have so many foods available from around the world, do you think it's good or bad for our traditions?

🔊 7.4

Sophie: Hello. I'm Sophie. This afternoon, I'm going to tell you about the results of my survey. My questions were on the topic of food and **culture** in France. I think this is an interesting topic. There were three questions in my survey.

The French love food and it's very important to them. So, my first question was, 'Is fast food popular in France?' I learned something really surprising. The French eat a lot of fast food; in fact it's their **favourite** food when eating out. You can see here that 54% of all restaurant sales were from fast food places. I didn't know it was so popular. In one survey I read, in the past, people had 80 minutes for lunch, but now only 22 minutes. Because lunches are shorter, people can't go home for **home-cooked meals**, so they eat fast food. I also read that more people eat alone or at their desks than they did before. My second question was, 'Is eating together with others important?' For most, 80% of the people, meals are still a time to eat and talk together.

My last question was, 'How do French people feel about food?' Scientists believe that feeling good about food is better for your health. So, when you look here, 84% of the people in France **enjoy** food. The taste is very important for French people. They eat **healthy** food like fresh fruits, vegetables, fish, meat and bread. Even fast food restaurants have to make meals that taste better than usual. Well, I wasn't surprised by that! Like everywhere, fast food is cheaper and easier for workers. So, my conclusion is, fast food is changing some traditions about eating in France. What do you think? Is fast food good or bad for our meal-time traditions?

🔊 7.5

Sophie: Hello. I'm Sophie. This afternoon, I'm going to tell you about the results of my survey. My questions were on the topic of food and culture in France. I think this is an interesting topic. There were three questions in my survey.

🔊 7.6

Tomoko: Good morning! I'm Tomoko. I'm going to tell you about the results of my survey. There were five questions in my survey. My topic was traditional Japanese food. I think this is an interesting topic.

Ahmed: Hello, everybody! I'm Ahmed. I'm going to tell you about the results of my survey. My topic was fast food in Jeddah. There were three questions in my survey. I think this is a good topic.

🔊 7.7

See script on page 166.

🔊 7.8

See script on page 166.

🔊 7.9

1 So, my first question was, 'Is fast food popular in France?'

2 You can see here that 54% percent of all restaurant sales were from fast food places.

3 In one survey I read, in the past, people had 80 minutes for lunch, but now only 22 minutes.

4 My second question was 'Is eating together with others important?'

5 My last question was, 'How do French people feel about food?'

6 So, when you look here, 84% of the people in France enjoy food …

UNIT 8

▶ China's modern roadways

More people have cars now than ever before. And the number is growing all the time.

As a result, there are also more roads than ever before. From Great Britain to Dubai, from the USA to Mexico, roads and highways will take you anywhere you want to go.

At the moment, China is constructing more roads than any other country in the world.

In 1989, China had fewer than 100 miles of highways. Now it has more than 50,000.

That's more than the United States, which has 47,000 miles of interstate highways.

In the middle of China, you can find one of the world's greatest roads.

It's called the G50.

The G50 is almost 1,200 miles long, and it connects the middle of China to the port city of Shanghai on the east coast.

It was difficult to build, but nothing could stop it. One minute you're driving through the middle of a mountain. The next minute you're driving in the air. This amazing highway also includes the world's highest bridge.

It's not this one.

It's this one, the Sidu Bridge.

The Sidu Bridge is more than 1,500 feet above the ground. It's so high that you could put the Empire State Building under it!

🔊 8.1

See script on page 176.

🔊 8.2

1435; 1749; 1949; 1953; 2017

🔊 8.3

Steve: Hi! Good morning! Thank you for asking me here today. OK, so my name's Steve, and I work for Transport for London. Today I'm going to tell you about the work we do and especially tell you about the electronic **tickets** we use in London.

OK, so what do we do at Transport for London? Well, we take care of travellers in London. This can be people who **travel** on private transport or public transport. Three million people travel in private cars and **taxis**, and another five million use the **bus**, **trains**, and, of course, the famous London Underground – which is the name of the world's oldest **metro**. So that's a total of around eight million people a day.

Student: How old is it?

Steve: Sorry? What was that?

Student: How old is the London Underground?

Steve: Ah! Oh, uh, it's more than 150 years old. It opened in 1863.

Student: Thanks.

Steve: So, Transport for London started in 2000, and, in 2003, we introduced the Oyster card. It's an electronic ticket system. Before Oyster cards, people had to buy paper tickets. And that was OK when fewer people lived and worked in London. They could buy tickets for one **journey** or for a day or for a month. But there was a problem – it was very slow.

Student: Why? How did people use tickets before?

Steve: Each **passenger** waited to buy a ticket and then they went to the gate. At the gate, they put the ticket into the machine. Then the gate opened and then they took their ticket from the machine. Now, this took a long time, and more people started to live and work in London, so we needed a faster ticket system. And this was the Oyster card. You can pay for your journeys online and walk through the gates much faster. Now, you can also use your credit card. You just tap your card. Or you can make a mobile payment with your phone. The result? It's very fast and easy. Many people are using this way to …

 8.4

See script on page 182.

 8.5

Teacher: OK, so work with your partner. Five minutes!

Iman: Hi, hello. I'm sorry. What's your name?

Anna: Oh, I'm Anna.

Iman: Anna? OK, and I'm Iman. Shall I go first?

Anna: Yes, sure. What's your topic?

Iman: Transport in cities: **problems** and solutions. OK, so I'm going to start with some facts about life in cities. More and more people are living in cities rather than in the countryside. This means that cities have a lot of **traffic** problems because many people use their cars to go to work or school or shop … or whatever. Many cities often have gridlock on the streets. That means the cars can't move. With all of these cars, it takes more time *and* **petrol** to travel around the city. This is expensive for people. Also, the smog is very bad in some places. Smog is a kind of air pollution. What's more, being in a car for a long time can be dangerous because drivers get tired. Traffic is a really tough problem. So, what is the solution?

Some cities think that bicycles are a good **idea**. They have bicycle-sharing schemes, so people can use bicycles for free. When there's a lot of traffic, cycling is sometimes quicker than driving. Other cities have car sharing. Car sharing means sharing journeys with other people. With car sharing, more people travel together in one car, so there aren't as many cars. There's another new idea that's interesting. It's a self-driving car. That means the car drives itself. That's right! People don't have to drive the car! And, because there are a lot of bad drivers, it can help stop **accidents**.

🔊 8.6

Now in the city of Dubai, they are working hard to find solutions for their traffic problems because there are too many cars. They plan to build a metro system – like the one in London – so there will be fewer cars on the road. Another thing is people don't like to walk on the **pavements** outside. It's too hot! So a big shopping centre there has an inside pavement, or walkway, that moves! Nice, huh? It's air-conditioned and goes from the shopping centre to the metro station and other places nearby. It's not short either. It takes 15–20 minutes to walk it, so people get exercise, feel comfortable and – more importantly – don't drive. These are some solutions some cities ...

🔊 8.7

Iman: More and more people are living in cities rather than in the countryside. This means that cities have a lot of traffic problems because many people use their cars to go to work or school or shop ... or whatever. Many cities often have gridlock on the streets. This means the cars can't move. With all of these cars, it takes more time *and* petrol to travel around the city. This is expensive for people. Also, the smog is very bad in some places.

🔊 8.8

Steve: Each passenger waited to buy a ticket and then they went to the gate. At the gate, they put the ticket into the machine. Then the gate opened and then they took their ticket from the machine. Now, this took a long time, and more people started to live and work in London, so we needed a faster ticket system. And this was the Oyster card.

🔊 8.9

See script on page 187.

ACKNOWLEDGEMENTS

The authors and publishers acknowledge the following sources of copyright material and are grateful for the permissions granted. While every effort has been made, it has not always been possible to identify the sources of all the material used, or to trace all copyright holders. If any omissions are brought to our notice, we will be happy to include the appropriate acknowledgements on reprinting and in the next update to the digital edition, as applicable.

Key: B = Below, C = Centre, L = Left, R = Right, T = Top, TL = Top Left, TR = Top Right, CL = Centre Left, CR = Centre Right, BL = Below Left, BR = Below Right, TC = Top Centre, BC = Below Centre.

Photos
All images are sourced from Getty Images.

p. 18 (L): ZouZou1/iStock/Getty Images Plus; p. 18 (R): Indeed; p. 21: Hill Street Studios/Blend Images; p. 25 (TL): Shirlaine Forrest/WireImage; p. 25 (TR): Neilson Barnard/Getty Images Entertainment; p. 25 (CL): Kimberly White/Getty Images Entertainment; p. 25 (CR): Paul Morigi/Getty Images Entertainment; p. 25 (BL): Michael Buckner/Getty Images Entertainment; p. 25 (BR): Patrick Riviere/Getty Images Entertainment; p. 27 (L): Kimberly White/Getty Images Entertainment; p. 27 (R): Bloomberg; pp. 36–37: Doug Lindstrand/Design Pics/First Light; p. 41 (TL), 43 (TL): New Saetiew/Moment Unreleased; p. 41 (TR), p. 43 (TR): Koichi Kamoshida/Getty Images News; p. 41 (BL), p. 43 (BL): kata716/iStock/Getty Images Plus; p. 41 (BR), p. 43 (BR): HasseChr/iStock Editorial/Getty Images Plus; p. 44 (TL): Education Images/Universal Images Group; p. 44 (TC): wastesoul/iStock/Getty Images Plus; p. 44 (TR): Eurasia/robertharding; p. 44 (BL): Arterra/Universal Images Group; p. 44 (BC): ED JONES/AFP; p. 44 (BR): SambaPhoto/Heloisa Passos; p. 48 (TL): Design Pics Inc/Perspectives; p. 48 (TR): Martin Siepmann/Westend61; p. 48 (BL): Allan Johnson/EyeEm; p. 48 (BR): Sirintra Pumsopa/Moment; p. 52 (L), p. 53 (L): prasit chansarekorn/E+; p. 52 (R), p. 53 (R): Benjamin Torode/Moment; pp. 58–59: David Sacks/Photographer's Choice; p. 62 (photo a): fstop123/iStock/Getty Images Plus; p. 62 (photo b): EmirMemedovski/E+; p. 62 (photo c): ColorBlind Images/The Image Bank; p. 63 (TL): JFB/Stone; p. 63 (TR): Betsie Van Der Meer/Taxi; p. 63 (BL): Kyle Sparks; p. 63 (BR): Robert Daly/Caiaimage; p. 65: Hero Images; p. 69: Michael H/DigitalVision; p. 71: Cathy Yeulet/Hemera; p. 72: marrio31/E+; p. 76: Nicola Tree/Photolibrary; pp. 80–81: mbbirdy/E+; p. 96: Betsie Van Der Meer/Taxi; pp. 102–103: Monty Rakusen/Cultura; p. 117 (L), p. 193 (L): Jupiterimages/Photolibrary; p. 117 (R), p. 195 (L): imagenavi; p. 121 (T), p. 122 (L): DreamPictures/Blend Images; p. 121 (C): Shannon Fagan/DigitalVision; p. 121 (B), p. 122 (R): David Sacks/Stone; pp. 126–127: Peter Adams/Photolibrary; p. 133 (armchair): Onur Döngel/E+; p. 133 (table): Bulgac/iStock/Getty Images Plus; p. 133 (chair): nuwatphoto/iStock/Getty Images Plus; p. 133 (bookcase): DEA/G. CIGOLINI/De Agostini; p. 133 (lamp): malerapaso/iStock/Getty Images Plus; p. 133 (desk): Spiderstock/E+; p. 133 (sofa): BLUEXHAND/iStock/Getty Images Plus; p. 135 (photo 1): Norman Hollands/Dorling Kindersley; p. 135 (photo 2): Peter Dazeley/Photographer's Choice; p. 135 (photo 3): Koukichi Takahashi/EyeEm; p. 135 (photo 4): Tinpixels/E+; p. 135 (photo 5): g-stockstudio/iStock/Getty Images Plus; p. 135 (photo 6): Buena Vista Images/DigitalVision; p. 135 (photo 7): Dovapi/iStock/Getty Images Plus; p. 139 (TL), p. 143 (L): Jean-Pierre Lescourret/Lonely Planet Images; p. 139 (TR), p. 143 (C): View Pictures/Universal Images Group; p. 139 (B), p. 143 (R): Pierre-Yves Babelon/Moment; pp. 148–149: Oleksiy Maksymenko/imageBROKER; p. 158 (photo 1): Thomas Firak Photography/Photographer's Choice; p. 158 (photo 2): Dorling Kindersley; p. 158 (photo 3): carlosgaw/E+; p. 158 (photo 4): Lilechka75/iStock/Getty Images Plus; p. 158 (photo 5): Elena_Danileiko/iStock/Getty Images Plus; p. 158 (photo 6): TAGSTOCK1/iStock/Getty Images Plus; p. 158 (photo 7): ElNariz/iStock/Getty Images Plus; p. 158 (photo 8): OksanaKiian/iStock/Getty Images Plus; pp. 170–171: Ellen van Bodegom/Moment; p. 176 (photo a): Travelpix Ltd/Photographer's Choice; p. 176 (photo b): geotrac/iStock/Getty Images Plus; p. 176 (photo c): David Crespo/iStock/Getty Images Plus; p. 176 (photo d): Bloomberg; p. 176 (photo e): helovi/iStock/Getty Images Plus; p. 178 (ferry): ruthyoel/DigitalVision Vectors; p. 179: Electra-K-Vasileiadou/iStock Editorial/Getty Images Plus; p. 189 (L): Jetta Productions/Blend Images; p. 189 (R): Ismailciydem/iStock/Getty Images Plus; p. 193 (R): Hiroyuki Matsumoto/Photographer's Choice; p. 195 (R): James Lauritz/Photographer's Choice RF.

The following images are from other libraries:
pp. 14–15: Derek Meijer/Alamy Stock Photo.

Front cover photography by Sino Images.

Video stills
All below stills are sourced from Getty Images.

p. 16 (video 1), p. 16 (video 3), p. 150: AFP Footage; p. 16 (video 2), p. 16 (video 4): Discovery FootageSource; p. 60 (video 1), p. 60 (video 2), p. 60 (video 3): Mark Kolbe/Getty Images Editorial Footage; p. 60 (video 4): Daniel Coolahan/Getty Images Editorial Footage.

The following stills are from other libraries:
p. 38, p. 82, p. 104, p. 128, p. 172: BBC Worldwide Learning.

Illustrations
p. 19, p. 107 (BR), p. 107 (TL), p. 107 (BC), p. 107 (TR), p. 114 (L), p. 114 (R): Ben Hasler (NB Illustration); p. 45, p. 85, p. 88, p. 89, p. 91, p. 92, p. 107 (TC), p. 114 (C), p. 107 (BL), p. 137, p. 140, p. 178, p. 181, p. 184: Oxford Designers & Illustrators; p. 87, p. 99, p. 100, p. 192, p. 194: Fiona Gowen.

Videos
All below clips are sourced from Getty Images and BBC Worldwide Learning.

Sky News/Film Image Partner; NewsHour Productions – Footage/Getty Images Editorial Footage; Eastfootage/Image Bank Film; Fuji Television Network, Inc./Image Bank Film; AFP Footage/AFP; Clippn/Getty Images Editorial Footage; Willem Viljoen, Teneighty/Image Bank Film; Mark Kolbe/Getty Images Editorial Footage; Daniel Coolahan/Getty Images Editorial Footage; Cordell Jigsaw Productions/Image Bank Film; davidf/Creatas Video; ifolio/Creatas Video+/Getty Images Plus; Ariel Skelley/Image Bank Film; Faithfulshot – Footage/Getty Images Editorial Footage; BBC Motion Gallery Editorial/BBC News/BBC Editorial; am1tk/iStock/Getty Images Plus; ullstein bild; Vividus/Creatas Video+/Getty Images Plus; FatCamera/Creatas Video; Travel Productions/Image Bank Film; Chuck and Sarah Fishbein/Iconica Video; primeimages/Creatas Video; Dorian Weber/Verve; Charles Yeo/Creatas Video+/Getty Images Plus; Bloomberg Video – Footage/Bloomberg; catchlights_sg/Creatas Video; Pavel Gospodinov/Image Bank Film; Pierre Ogeron/Photodisc; BBC Worldwide Learning.

Corpus
Development of this publication has made use of the Cambridge English Corpus (CEC). The CEC is a multi-billion word computer database of contemporary spoken and written English. It includes British English, American English and other varieties of English. It also includes the Cambridge Learner Corpus, developed in collaboration with the University of Cambridge ESOL Examinations. Cambridge University Press has built up the CEC to provide evidence about language use that helps to produce better language teaching materials.

Cambridge Dictionaries
Cambridge dictionaries are the world's most widely used dictionaries for learners of English. The dictionaries are available in print and online at dictionary.cambridge.org. Copyright © Cambridge University Press, reproduced with permission.

Typeset by emc design ltd.

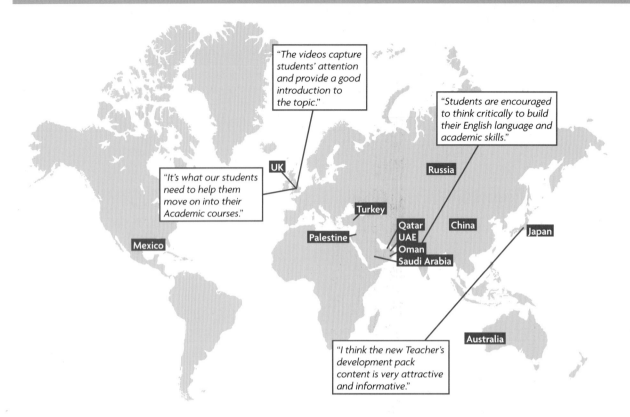

"The videos capture students' attention and provide a good introduction to the topic."

"Students are encouraged to think critically to build their English language and academic skills."

"It's what our students need to help them move on into their Academic courses."

"I think the new Teacher's development pack content is very attractive and informative."

UK
Russia
Turkey
Mexico
Palestine
Qatar
UAE
Oman
Saudi Arabia
China
Japan
Australia

We would like to thank the following ELT professionals all around the world for their support, expertise and input throughout the development of *Unlock* Second Edition:

Adnan Abu Ayyash, Birzeit University, Palestine	Takayuki Hara, Kagoshima University, Japan	Megan Putney, Dhofar University, Oman
Bradley Adrain, University of Queensland, Australia	Esengül Hasdemir, Atilim University, Turkey	Wayne Rimmer, United Kingdom
Sarah Ali, Nottingham Trent International College (NTIC), United Kingdom	Irina Idilova, Moscow Institute of Physics and Technology, Russia	Sana Salam, TED University, Turkey
Ana Maria Astiazaran, Colegio Regis La Salle, Mexico	Meena Inguva, Sultan Qaboos University, Oman	Setenay Şekercioglu, Işık University, Turkey
Asmaa Awad, University of Sharjah, United Arab Emirates	Vasilios Konstantinidis, Prince Sultan University, Kingdom of Saudi Arabia	Robert B. Staehlin, Morioka University, Japan
Jesse Balanyk, Zayed University, United Arab Emirates	Andrew Leichsenring, Tamagawa University, Japan	Yizhi Tang, Xueersi English, TAL Group, China
Lenise Butler, Universidad del Valle de México, Mexico	Alexsandra Minic, Modern College of Business and Science, Oman	Valeria Thomson, Muscat College, Oman
Esin Çağlayan, Izmir University of Economics, Turkey	Daniel Newbury, Fuji University, Japan	Amira Traish, University of Sharjah, United Arab Emirates
Matthew Carey, Qatar University, Qatar	Güliz Özgürel, Yaşar University, Turkey	Poh Leng Wendelkin, INTO City, University of London, United Kingdom
Eileen Dickens, Universidad de las Américas, Mexico	Özlem Perks, Istanbul Ticaret University, Turkey	Yoee Yang, The Affiliated High School of SCNU, China
Mireille Bassam Farah, United Arab Emirates	Claudia Piccoli, Harmon Hall, Mexico	Rola Youhia, University of Adelaide College, Australia
Adriana Ghoul, Arab American University, Palestine	Tom Pritchard, University of Edinburgh, United Kingdom	Long Zhao, Xueersi English, TAL Group, China
Burçin Gönülsen, Işık University, Turkey		